# LEST WE FORGET

Thirty years ago, on the 10th anniversary of
the Allied invasion of Europe, the *Daily Express*
published this graphic account of the D-Day
landings as a tribute to the valour of the men
who took part. We are equally proud to
reproduce it now, to mark the 40th anniversary
of those landings. Nothing has been
changed, nothing added. It is as forceful, and
as meaningful now as it was then.

Sir Larry Lamb
Editor
The *Daily Express*
May 1984

©1984 Express Newspapers Plc., 121 Fleet Street, London EC4P 4JT
First published 1954: This edition published 1984.
Printed by R. J. Acford, Chichester, Sussex, England.  Reproduction by Hallmark Graphics. Co-ordinated by Roeder Print Services Ltd.

UK Price £1.95

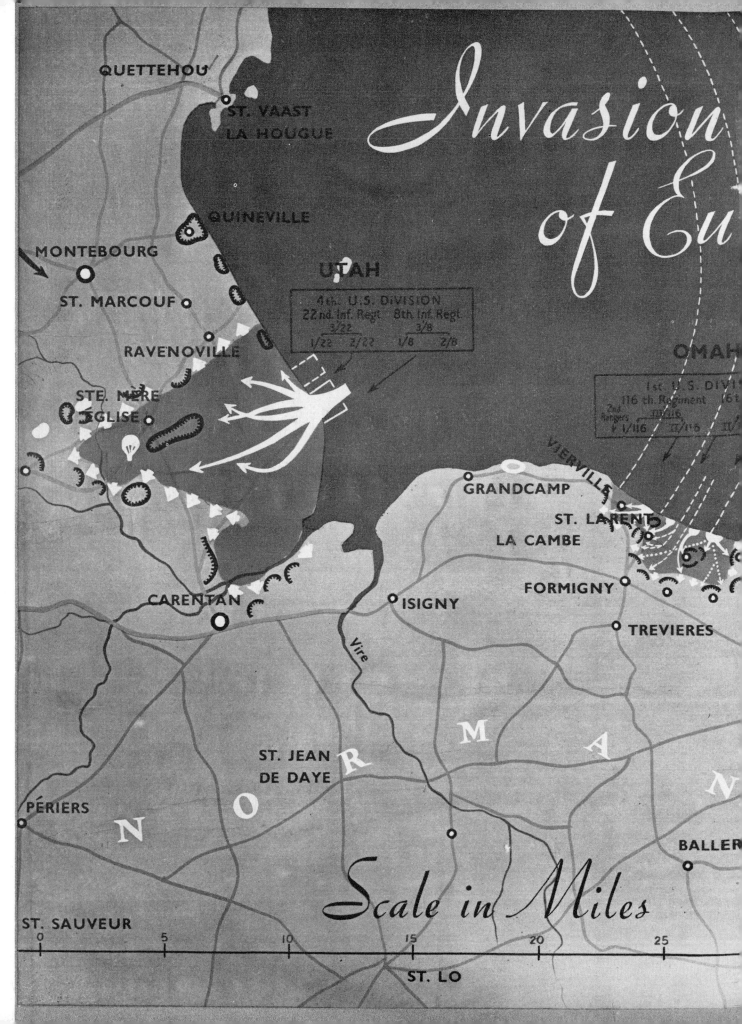

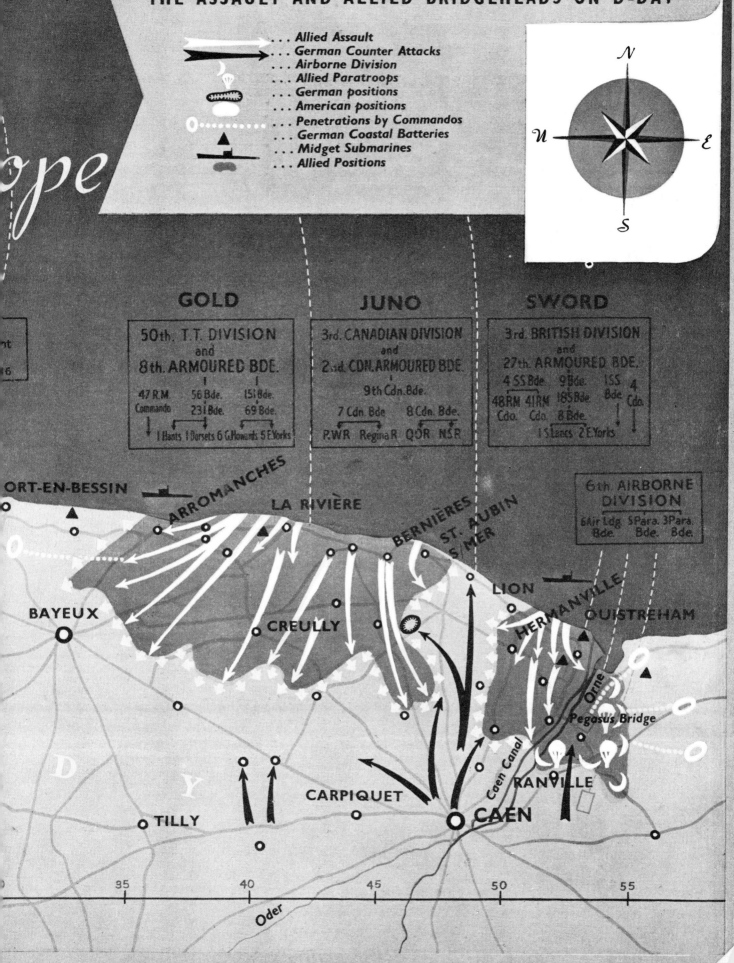

# THE ASSAULT AND ALLIED BRIDGEHEADS ON D-DAY

- . . . **Allied Assault**
- . . . **German Counter Attacks**
- . . . **Airborne Division**
- . . . **Allied Paratroops**
- . . . **German positions**
- . . . **American positions**
- . . . **Penetrations by Commandos**
- . . . **German Coastal Batteries**
- . . . **Midget Submarines**
- . . . **Allied Positions**

*ope*

**GOLD**

| 50th. T.T. DIVISION |
| and |
| 8th. ARMOURED BDE. |

| 47 R.M. | 56 Bde. | 151 Bde. |
| Commando | 231 Bde. | 69 Bde. |

1 Hants 1 Dorsets 6 G.Howards 5 E.Yorks

**JUNO**

| 3rd. CANADIAN DIVISION |
| and |
| 2nd. CDN. ARMOURED BDE. |

9th Cdn. Bde.

| 7 Cdn. Bde. | 8 Cdn. Bde. |

P.W.R Regina R QOR N.S.R.

**SWORD**

| 3rd. BRITISH DIVISION |
| and |
| 27th. ARMOURED BDE. |

| 4 SS Bde. | 9 Bde. | 1 SS Bde. | 4 Cdo. |
| 48 RM 41 RM | 185 Bde. | |
| Cdo. Cdo. | 8 Bde. | |

1 S Lancs 2 E.Yorks

| 6th. AIRBORNE DIVISION |
| 6 Air Ldg. | 5 Para. | 3 Para. |
| Bde. | Bde. | Bde. |

ARROMANCHES

ORT-EN-BESSIN

LA RIVIÈRE

BERNIÈRES

ST. AUBIN S/MER

BAYEUX

CREULLY

LION

HERMANVILLE

OUISTREHAM

Orne

Pegasus Bridge

Caen Canal

RANVILLE

CARPIQUET

TILLY

**CAEN**

D  Y

Oder

35    40    45    50    55

WITH pride the *Daily Express* publishes this book on the 10th Anniversary of "D" Day. Herein is portrayed the valour and sacrifice of free men who took part in this great invasion for the liberation of Europe.

The *Daily Express* acknowledges the valuable help from the following official sources which made this memorable book possible :—

The Department of the Chief of Naval Information ; the Public Relations Branch, the War Office ; the Air Historical Branch, the Air Ministry ; Brigadier Latham, the Cabinet Office ; the U.S. Army Attache ; Captain Chambliss, U.S. Navy ; Captain Golding, the Canadian Army Liaison Establishment ; Alfred J. Charge and the Staff of the Photographic Branch, Imperial War Museum ; The Institution of Mechanical Engineers.

*Published in London in June 1954 by*
BEAVERBROOK NEWSPAPERS LIMITED

●

*Written and compiled by*
JOHN ST. JOHN COOPER

●

*Designed and Produced by*
EDWARD L. MATTO

●

# INVASION!

## The D-DAY story

### JUNE 6 · 1944

# LEST WE

ON the 6th June, 1944, ten years ago, a great Allied Force landed on the coast of Normandy. Many of us had been in France earlier in the war, in the Dunkirk campaign ; I had myself, and I left on the night of 31st May, 1940.

*This* time we were all imbued with one single aim : we had come back to stay, and our task now was to deal the Germans a shattering blow and win the war as quickly as possible.

We knew the invasion landing would be difficult ; but I had complete confidence that we would succeed. We had on our side the great asset of surprise ; we also had the benefit of meticulous planning and rehearsing, great concentration of strength, and a big advantage in morale.

I issued orders to the land armies that the objectives for D-Day must be the deepest which it was possible for the troops to reach. D-Day was the attackers day. Leading troops were to go straight for their furthest objectives, irrespective of the situation on their flanks ; they must " peg out " claims inland. In my orders to the armies I said :

" It may take weeks to get the ground you fail to get on D-Day. It does not matter how ragged the dispositions are at the end of D-Day ; they can be sorted out on D+1."

And how magnificently the soldiers responded !

Such a vast operation could never have succeeded without the closest cooperation between land, sea, and air forces. This was achieved ; under the overall direction and command of General Eisenhower, the Allied Forces were welded into a magnificent fighting machine.

These pictures tell the story of the invasion and of the fighting during the battle of Normandy. It is a story of human endeavour by British and Allied fighting men that will long shine in history. But do not let us forget that many brave men gave their lives that we who remain might have freedom and a better world.

We have been at peace now for over nine years. Possibly some of us are inclined to forget all that happened between September 1939 and May 1945, and to

# of ALAMEIN
# FORGET

forget WHY it happened. We must not forget.

This is the least we can do for the brave fighting men who gave their lives that we might win through to Victory.

When the German war was over I issued an Order of the Day to the British Group of Armies from my Headquarters on Luneburg Heath, dated 8th May, 1945. In that Order I said :

> " Great problems lie ahead ; the world will not recover quickly from the upheaval that has taken place ; there is much work for each one of us.

> We have won the German war. Let us now win the peace."

Have we won the peace ? No. It can be won, but only if we understand two things.

*First.* On the home front, in the dark days of the war we all drew close together and we realized how dependent we were on one another. Do not let us forget that in modern times this is necessary *in peace* just as much as in war.

*Second.* On the international front, we must remember that true unity between a group of nations in peace time is impossible without some sacrifices on the part of each for the common good ; the key to collective strength is unselfish solidarity. In the hand of strength lie the keys of peace : religious strength, moral strength, economic strength and military strength.

Having read this book and studied the pictures, I feel sure we shall go forward with confidence towards our objective of lasting peace : free, united and strong.

*Montgomery of Alamein.*

F.M.

A FEW months after Dunkirk, even when the invasion of our own shores seemed imminent, Mr. Churchill ordered the Joint Planning Staff to consider plans to attack Nazi occupied Europe, and establish a bridgehead on the Cotentin peninsula.

Time passed.

The Battle of Britain was won by 'the Few'. With Lord Beaverbrook in charge of aircraft production the strength of the R.A.F. increased with incredible speed. The Luftwaffe became outnumbered and out-dated : we gained superiority in the air.

Lease Lend began and subsequently Japan and America entered the war. At sea there was the desperate struggle between Allied convoys and Nazi U-boats. In 1942 six million tons of merchant shipping were sunk by Admiral Doenitz's submarines. It was the scientists who turned the tide of battle. Aircraft carriers and long range shore based aircraft carrying special radar equipment covered the Atlantic and soon our shipping losses were one-tenth of what they had been previously and the U-boat packs were driven off the seas. In 1943 the Battle of the Atlantic had been won.

Meanwhile Britain had become a fortress, a mighty fortress ready to launch an attack. General Morgan had prepared an invasion plan coded ' Cossac '. From a plan it became a reality. General Eisenhower was appointed Supreme Commander, Admiral Ramsay to command the Allied Navies, General Montgomery the Allied Armies and Air Chief Marshal Leigh-Mallory the Allied Air Forces. Amendments were made to ' Cossac ', and the result was **' Overlord ',** the plan to invade and liberate Europe.

The time was ripe to launch the Second Front.

# TOP SECRET "Overlord"

**ONE WAY TRAFFIC.** Side by side, tanks and Dukws block the road as the 2nd Army moves to the coast ready to embark on landing craft of the Western Task Force. Sealed off, the entire south coast of England was like a vast military camp.

IN the spring of 1944 all Britain was tense. It was almost something tangible, like the heat or cold it could be felt. In factories, docks, offices, and in the fields people worked feverishly with a will to get things done.

·Everyone sensed that the invasion was near, but no one knew when it would be launched or where it would strike.

From the Highlands of Scotland, where they had been training all winter, to those stationed on the tip of Cornwall, the troops were unsettled, waiting. Units were alive with rumours of " we're moving" and, for once, there was more authority for the guesses than the C.O's. batman, or the latrine orderly. Eventually the orders came through and, amid farewells from the local people where they had been stationed, the troops entrained and the great move South began.

Overnight vast camps sprang up along the coast right from South Wales to the Wash. Train-load after train-load of troops and vehicles began to

**TRY OUT.** Through King Street, 'somewhere in the south of England', a tank returns to camp after a final 'scheme' prior to the briefing and loading for the actual invasion.

**BRIEFING.** Rugged-faced Commandos listen intently to their commander. There is no bravado, they know the risks, they are not afraid.

**" ON THE RUN IN . . ."** Three weeks before D-Day young Naval officers are thoroughly instructed in the part which they are to play.

"KNIFE, FORK, SPOON, RAZOR . . ." In the concentration areas kit is checked to ensure that every item is complete.

arrive at hundreds of small stations ; armoured brigades thundered through the countryside : the greatest military machine of all time was concentrating.

At top levels there were frantic amendments and alterations to the plans. There was one final exercise, a 'cushy' one compared to those in the chill sea and snowclad mountains of Scotland. Then, for the troops, there was waiting . . . just waiting.

For a while there was freedom, week-end passes, afternoons off, and trips down to the local pubs—when there was any beer. The men wrote home, played cards, pitch-and-toss—both military offences but now passed with a blind eye.

Suddenly the camps were sealed overnight. With barbed wire all round and guards posted, no one was allowed in or out—they became 'just like ruddy concentration camps'.

Then briefing began ; slow, careful, methodical briefing on large scale maps and aerial photographs until each man knew the coast-line thoroughly and had

WEIGHT PROBLEM. With Major Tighe-Wood and Col. Harris, General Montgomery checks the kit a rifleman is supposed to carry. The 'guinea pig' is Rfn. McCracken of the Ulsters.

**THE FLEET WAITS.** Laying six deep alongside the jetty, infantry and tank landing craft are covered with camouflage netting ready for loading.

**BACK UP!** Straight from the beach a tank of a British Armoured Brigade backs up carefully into a L.S.T. of the Western Task Force.

**OPEN SESAME.** The giant doors of a tank landing ship are open as an American tank manœuvres on the quay ready to load on board.

memorised the route off the beach to his unit's assembly area. Platoon commanders even selected houses on the outskirts of Caen for their platoon H.Qs. Everyone was thoroughly 'in the picture'.

Meanwhile along the coast the invasion fleet moved up ready for loading.

In the camps new anti-vermin battle-dresses were issued to the troops and all their other belongings, except the kit and equipment they would carry into action, were handed in to be delivered later in France. Some had the bright idea of parcelling up a spare shirt and underclothes, addressing the parcel to themselves c/o the British Liberation Army, and handing them over to the camp staff for posting once the invasion was launched.

Time was growing short. From the camps the troops moved to transit areas where they were split into boat-loads and then proceeded down to the embarkation points.

There, in tents, barrack-rooms, and in the open, the vast armies waited while loud-speakers blared the numbers of the various boatloads. As each number was called men heaved into their kit, paraded, and marched off over the deserted promenades and beaches to the ships.

Toiling and sweating they stumbled along the gangways on to the small assault craft which, when filled, cast off and waited. . . .

**HOIST AWAY!** Transport of the 51st Highland Division is loaded on to a cargo ship.

**MIND MY BIKE!** Laden with kit, and carrying folding bicycles, Commandos stagger down the gangway on to a waiting assault craft.

**ALL ABOARD.** It is D minus 1. Carrier crews of the 3rd Division wait expectantly for the landing craft to sail.

**BOATS WITH A BITE.** Vicious-looking motor torpedo boats of the coastal forces lie waiting for the signal to cast off.

**G.I. INVADERS.** Over deserted beaches, closed for security, American assault infantry file on to landing craft of the Eastern Task Force.

**WHY ARE WE WAITING?** Assault craft lay off the mother ship waiting to be hoisted aboard. Tomorrow the waiting will be over.

# "GOD SPEED"

**LINE AHEAD.** Assault landing craft of Force G. commanded by Cmdr. C. E. Douglas-Pennant, wheel into formation with drill-like precision before steaming past the Headquarters ships of the invasion which are drawn up in line in the background.

**ROYAL SALUTE.** The King stands alone to take the salute as the tiny craft sweep speedily past. His signal is "God speed," and every man in the fleet knows full well that the invasion day is near at hand.

**NOTHING IS UNIFORM** but courage and service. Clutching caps, trilbys and bowlers, men of the Merchant Navy proudly honour their King. Perhaps they look a little strange—they feel it ; but manning the landing ships they were in their element.

**EYES FRONT.** Shoulder to shoulder 'rookies' and old salts stand rigidly to attention as the King, himself an old sailor, inspects ratings of the cruiser H.M.S. *Scylla*. This was in the home waters of the Solent when D-Day was still some weeks away, but already the Navy is ready for action.

**GOD SAVE THE KING.** The King is about to leave his fleet. The Marines present arms, the ships' officers salute as the band strikes up the National Anthem. On the gangway H.M. the King stands alone : he who gave so much in the service of his peoples.

# Air Conquest

**TAKE OFF.** In the dusk lights wink out, men of the ground crew signal and a Lancaster roars on to the runway. Behind it another throttles forward impatiently waiting its turn to take-off.

THE war in the air was over long before D-Day. It was a far call back to 1940 when, fighting alone, Britain had been saved from invasion by the gallant band of pilots whose name is immortal as " The Few "

Since then the R.A.F. had doubled, trebled and quadrupled—there had been no shortage of aircrews : Lord Beaverbrook produced the planes. Vast American Air Forces operated from Britain, the mighty Flying Fortresses striking into the heart of Germany. In the spring of 1944, Goering's Luftwaffe was a shattered force hunted and harried whenever it dared to take to the air.

Top priority for the Allied Air Forces in the invasion was the wrecking of enemy lines of communication to prevent the Germans bringing up reinforcements before the armies in the bridgehead were sufficiently firmly established to meet a major counter-attack. This meant wrecking the French railway system. Junctions, depots, and repair and maintenance centres became the pre-D-Day objectives for the strategic air forces.

Eighty main railway targets in Belgium and Northern France were selected and during March the raids began.

**TARGET NORMANDY.** Nearly a hundred Lancasters of Bomber Command fly over the Channel in daylight to attack enemy concentrations. These raids delayed the V-bombs starting.

Day and night heavy bombers took off to blast the targets. Later they were followed by medium and fighter bombers which harassed and prevented repair work being done.

By the dawn of D-Day rail traffic in France had been reduced to one quarter, V-bomb sites had been attacked and few of the enemy Channel radar stations were still in operation. All the bridges across the Seine between Rouen and Paris were blocked by the Allied tactical air forces.

As May turned into June aircraft of Coastal Command roved over the sea to prevent U-boats breaking into the Channel and to ward off E-boats and other enemy surface craft. Over a thousand bombers were loaded to attack enemy coastal batteries ; fighters were ready to take off and give cover to the Allied Armada, carry out patrols, do reconnaissance for General Montgomery's H.Q., and observe naval gunfire. Dakotas, Halifaxes and Albemarles stood waiting for the airborne troops to load.

The Air Force had paved the way for the army and was now ready to help in the assault.

**ALL SERENE.** A patrol of Spitfires flies unchallenged. Their battle was won long ago by ' the Few '. *Below* American Flying Fortresses fly towards France, their fighter escort weaving a pattern of vapour trails in the sky as though in defiance of the Luftwaffe who could not intercept them

**BOMBS AWAY.** The bomb bays gape as an R.A.F. Lancaster drops its deadly cargo through the clouds on to an objective in northern France.

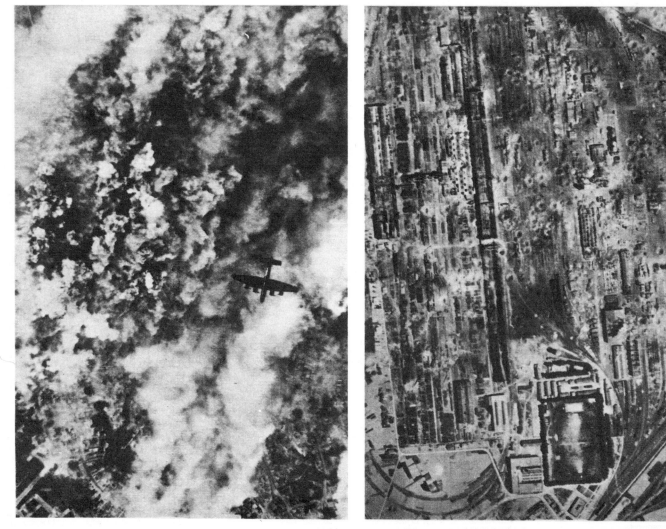

**PALL OF DEATH.** A Lancaster turns home as, beneath it, the target area flames and smoulders—destroyed by the accurate bombing.

**PATTERN OF DESTRUCTION.** This was Chambly, one of the most vital railway depots in France, after a heavy R.A.F. attack in May.

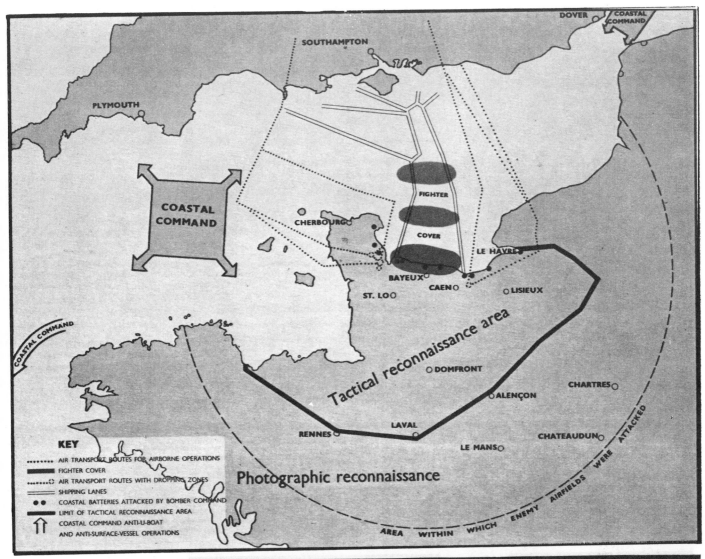

COASTAL COMMAND

PLYMOUTH

SOUTHAMPTON

DOVER
COASTAL COMMAND

COASTAL COMMAND

CHERBOURG

FIGHTER

COVER

LE HAVRE

BAYEUX

CAEN

LISIEUX

ST. LO

Tactical reconnaissance area

DOMFRONT

CHARTRES

ALENÇON

LAVAL

CHATEAUDUN

RENNES

LE MANS

Photographic reconnaissance

AREA WITHIN WHICH ENEMY AIRFIELDS WERE ATTACKED

**KEY**

· · · · · · AIR TRANSPORT ROUTES FOR AIRBORNE OPERATIONS
━━━━━ FIGHTER COVER
· · · ·○ AIR TRANSPORT ROUTES WITH DROPPING ZONES
━━━━━ SHIPPING LANES
●● COASTAL BATTERIES ATTACKED BY BOMBER COMMAND
━ ━ ━ LIMIT OF TACTICAL RECONNAISSANCE AREA
⇑ COASTAL COMMAND ANTI-U-BOAT
   AND ANTI-SURFACE-VESSEL OPERATIONS

## JUNE 6, 1944

This map shows the complete air coverage for the assault on Europe —the direct fighter cover over the Allied Armada and the beachhead ; the coastal command patrols guarding against U-boats and enemy naval craft ; and the tactical and photographic reconnaissance areas. The latter were invaluable to Army and Corps commanders in assessing the disposition of the enemy forces.

**BOMB BAYS OPEN.** Leaving a vapour trail behind, a Flying Fortress of the Eighth U.S. Air Force nears the target. Poised in the racks are the huge bombs which, seconds after this picture was taken, were crashing down to blast Nazi-occupied Europe.

**TWO HEADS.** General Eisenhower the Supreme Commander listens thoughtfully to General Montgomery Commander-in-Chief of the Allied Armies.

# The VITAL DECISION

IT was four o'clock in the morning of Sunday, June 4, two hours before the assault forces were due to sail. In a room at Southwick Park behind Portsmouth, the Allied commanders listened gloomily to the weather report—the forecast of a storm. There was no alternative but to postpone the invasion for twenty-four hours, from June 5 to June 6. History had been altered by the weather.

During the day the storm raged and that evening when the Allied commanders met again a wild wind whistled outside the windows of the conference room. But the report was better. The weather over the Atlantic was unsettled, but improving.

Eisenhower, Tedder, Montgomery, Ramsay, Leigh-Mallory faced the situation knowing that a further postponement would mean a fortnight's delay for a suitable day. Each stated his views then Eisenhower made the vital decision : " O.K. Let's go."

# Airborne Spearhead

**PEP TALK.** Having made the vital decision Eisenhower has a final word with American paratroops before they load into the transport planes.

THE night was cool with the gentleness of early summer, but the serene beauty of it passed unnoticed: the men on the airfields were too pre-occupied.

There was a call, " Oi, N.A.A.F.I. up ! " as a mobile canteen pulled up beside the aircraft and men swarmed round, men grown grotesque with faces streaked with black and green, each a one-man army so laden were they with guns, knives, ammunition and grenades.

They were the spearhead of the Invasion, the paratroops and glider-borne infantry of General Gale's 6th Airborne Division who were to drop over Normandy in the early hours of D-Day.

Their task was vital—to seize and hold the bridges over the River Orne and the Caen Canal on the open east flank of the British Liberation Army. Here would fall the full might of the German panzer counter-attack which, if it got through, could thrust right through the British beachhead.

On the extreme west flank the Americans were to drop, the 101st

**STEADY** . . . Carefully a jeep is loaded into a glider. Anti-tank guns were also flown over.

**D MINUS I.** 'Sticks' of paratroops are carried in lorries to the transports all ready to turn in to the runway. The invasion is on.

Division to hold the line of the River Douve and the Carentan Canal, the 82nd Division to drop astride the River Merderet and open up the route for an early drive across the Cherbourg peninsula.

Each man had been thoroughly ' put in the picture ', they knew the task and they knew the dangers. Now, waiting to load, they talked and joked, each man striving to avoid being alone with his own thoughts . . .

" 'Ere, sarge, don't make us swim for it—my missus says the water isn't really warmed through till August."

The sergeant glider pilot grinned : " I should worry—I can't swim." With the weight of kit each of them carried

both would have sunk in an instant in the sea. But that didn't occur to them.

" Righto, chaps. Fall in."

This was it. The men formed a line —a thousand lines on half-a-dozen airfields—and were finally inspected by their commanders as they clambered aboard the planes and gliders.

Soon there was a raucous cough that spluttered into a roar as the first aircraft taxied to the runways.

Lights winked out and the planes rolled gathering speed to take off.

Ahead of the main body were the paratroop pathfinders and a small group of six gliders. The pathfinders were to mark out the DZs—dropping zones—for the main body, and then

reinforce the infantry and R.Es. in the six gliders who were to swoop down silently, crash land and seize the Orne bridges, and then hold them until reinforcements arrived.

Hardly had the drone of the aircraft carrying this small vital force died out when a mightier noise took its place— the concerted throb of over a thousand transport planes taking off with the main body of paratroops. In a seemingly unending stream they gained height and headed South.

In a little while the night was deserted and peaceful again but for the heavy throb that lingered in the air, heavy like the thunder of an approaching storm.

**WAR PAINT.** Paratroops, their faces blackened, enjoy the message chalked on a glider . . . a message to be delivered in person.

**IT IS EXACTLY . . .** Four officers specially selected for the vital job of pathfinders, synchronise their watches with their commander before take-off

**ALL SET.** Watched by the R.A.F. crew, the paratroops clamber aboard. They are the spearhead of the liberation army. Out of the darkness they will bring the light of freedom to the peoples of Europe.

**THEY FOLLOWED.** Gliders of the air landing brigade ready to take off to reinforce the hard-pressed left flank of the bridgehead.

**TWO UP.** The plane roars down the runway . . . the tow is taut . . . suddenly the glider is airborne. They are committed, only the plane will return. In the darkness inside the glider there is nothing for the infantry to do but sit and wait.

On the bridge of H.M.S. *Holmes* all eyes are strained ahead, not a glance is spared the Allied airborne armada which was passing overhead.

# The Armada Under Way

While barrage balloons hover above in the summer sky, tank landing craft leave England. Amongst the cargo are vehicles of a Field Ambulance unit.

THE decision was made. June 6 was to be D-Day.

Along the entire South Coast top secret signals flashed to Naval commanders from Admiral Ramsay, the Allied Naval Commander-in-Chief.

Early on June 5 the fleet put to sea—some ships for the second time in two days.

Earlier, before the invasion had been put back twenty-four hours, a part of Force O from Portland, and Force U from Devonshire, both carrying American troops destined to land on Utah and Omaha beaches, had set off and had to be recalled. One slow convoy of 128 L.c.Ts. with their escort were only turned back when finally reached by a Walrus flying boat and two destroyers.

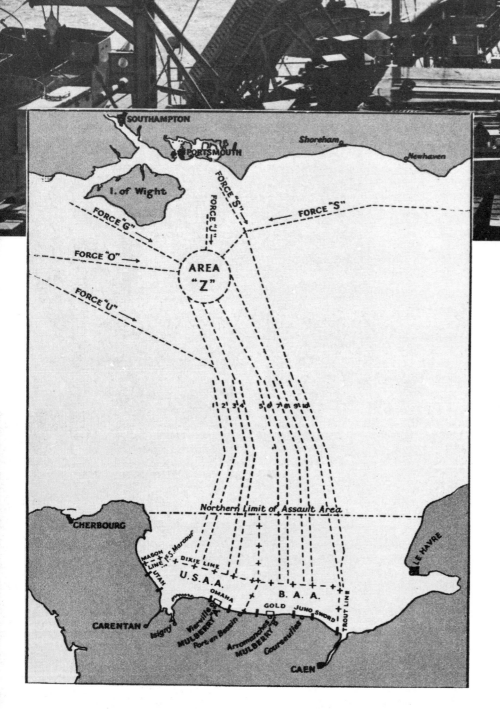

Had they not been contacted when they were they would soon have been detected by enemy radar, the French coast would have been alerted, and the whole operation endangered.

As the ships slipped out of the shelter of the harbours the weather was still bad with gusty winds whipping the Channel into waves five to six feet high. Some of the minor landing craft were so buffetted that they had to turn back to harbour. They contained units that were to have landed on the afternoon of D-Day. None of the assault forces were delayed. They steamed ahead towards their goal—Normandy.

On board the vast fleet of ships and landing craft the troops lined up with their mess tins for steaming stew and plum pudding, the 'buckshee' rations left over being shared out between platoons and stuffed—God knows how —into already bulging haversacks.

Down the English coast the small ships heaved and rolled. Men yawned, turned pale and clenched their teeth, then edged their way determinedly along gangways to their platoon commanders for sea-sickness pills. Then they headed for their bunks.

Soon there was an unreal quiet over the whole fleet. For four years the sea had been Britain's greatest ally. Now it was a foe. The vast allied armies were pale and stricken with sickness. This was the Navies' job, and they did it magnificently. Destroyers sped around the fleet like sheep dogs, hurrying, harrying and always protecting. Away ahead the gallant, ugly minesweepers bucked through the rising sea clearing lanes for the armada.

From Harwich to the Bristol Channel the craft converged on " Piccadilly Circus "—officially ' **Area Z** '—a circular sea area some eight miles in diameter, fifteen miles south-east of the Isle of Wight. Here the fleet massed until darkness when it could proceed on its course, hidden from enemy reconnaissance.

The Eastern Task Force, composed of the British and Canadians sailed from Southampton, Portsmouth, the Solent and Spithead to assault the eastern beaches—Sword, Juno and Gold. Meanwhile, embarked at Dartmouth, Salcombe, Weymouth, and a dozen other smaller ports, the American Western Task Force were to land to the west on Omaha and Utah beaches.

Darkness fell. The fleet headed majestically south.

Aboard the Headquarters' ship last-minute conferences were held, final orders were issued, the fleet steadied. In the tiny wardrooms of the L.c.Is. company commanders studied their maps with their platoon commanders. The men, cramped below deck, played cards or turned in. Worst off were those in the flat-bottomed L.c.Ts. which heaved, pitched and rolled ; nor was there any shelter from the weather—only sleep was merciful.

In the small hours of the night there was a giant roar in the air as the airborne troops passed over. The officers of the watch grinned, reassured. Soon they were past and the night was still again.

Farther north of the main invasion fleet a small convoy with special barrage balloons flying, edged towards the Pas de Calais. With accompanying aircraft their object was to be detected by the enemy radar and give the impression that it was there the landings were to be made.

**GOD SPEED.** Still at anchor, a Headquarters ship gets up steam as L.c.Ts. sail past under way.

**OPEN SEA.** There is no sign of enemy aircraft as the convoy sweeps out into the Channel.

**PARLEZ VOUS . . .** Men of the R.E.M.E., their ' Mae Wests ' tied on ready for an emergency, waste no time punching up their French. Their spirits are high as the craft gets under way. They know what tomorrow holds, but they will not fail.

The hours slipped by. The armada neared the coast of Normandy. Tension grew as they got closer, but there was no murmur from the enemy coastal guns and, as Admiral Ramsay commented : " the realisation that complete tactical surprise had been achieved slowly dawned."

With the first light of day came action. The quiet was shattered by ear-splitting crashes as salvo after salvo was fired at the coastal defences.

The whole Channel seemed to erupt as the bombardment began.

In one salvo from her 16-in. guns H.M.S. *Nelson* poured eight tons of shells on to enemy positions. Swarms of destroyers swept close in to the shore firing at point blank range at whatever targets presented themselves. The *Warspite, Nelson, Belfast, Frobisher, Ceres*—all opened up at the shore.

Overhead the bombers droned above the beaches raining bombs on the shore batteries and enemy strongpoints. Fighters, wheeling, diving, climbing, observed the fire of the naval guns and signalled back to the battleships and cruisers.

On the left flank a smoke screen was laid across the sea to hide the ships from the powerful coastal batteries at Le Havre. Three E-boats slipped through it to investigate only to turn violently back when they found themselves so close to the capital ships of the Navy.

Reaching the lowering positions the mother ships drew up ready for the assault troops to be loaded into the L.c.As. and lowered into the sea for the run-in to the beaches.

The invaders were ready. H-hour was at hand.

ABANDON SHIP. A direct hit just forward of the bridge turns a large vessel of the fleet into a blazing hulk in a matter of minutes. (*Inset right*) Seen from an R.A.F. plane, assault craft head for the beach.

**TAKING NO CHANCES.** The sea erupts in the wake of H.M.S. *Holmes* as a depth charge explodes on a suspected U-Boat. With the R.A.F. masters of the sky, mines and U-Boats were the greatest menaces to the invasion fleet.

**ACTION!** H.M.S. *Rodney* opens fire on enemy shore positions while (*below*) the French Frigate *La Suprise* moves in to support the assault.

**MARKERS.** Two of these tiny 'X' craft lay just off the French coast and signalled the directions to the first assault wave going in.

**LOOK OUT.** A.B. Rae scans the beaches as the assault troops fight for a hold on the beaches.

**THE INVADERS.** Crouched in their tiny assault craft, the first infantry ride through the dawn to the raging inferno that awaits them ahead on the beaches.

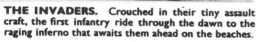

**BRASS HATS.** Aboard an M.L., Admiral Cunningham and Air Vice Marshal Portal watch the progress.

**"GOOD LADS!"** General Graham, G.O.C. of the 50th (Northumbrian) Division watches anxiously as his two leading brigades hit the beach and go forward into action.

# TOUCH DOWN

**MORNING MIST** covers the beach as tanks of the 13/18th Hussars touch down near a guiding flare. Behind them mined beach obstacles jut out menacingly above the waves.

**R.A.F. VIEW.** Landing craft nose in to unload assault troops who immediately dash to attack.

IN the chill first light of dawn the assault craft were lowered from the mother ships between seven and ten miles off shore.

The men were gaunt, only their set jaws betraying emotion. Their wills were made, letters—for some their last —had been written and handed over to the ships' crews.

Clumsy under their masses of kit they squeezed into the L.c.As. There was a soft " Damn ! " as a rifle clanged against the brim of a steel helmet. Someone said, " What price Southend? " in a forced voice. No one answered.

As the assault companies cast off cheers rang out from the fleet : a bugler of the East Yorks sounded the General Salute. It was acknowledged by the Admiral and the Divisional Commander. Each man felt a chill of pride. It was a stirring moment.

But within minutes the unreal security of the mother ship was part of the past. The small craft were under way, the sea alive with them, heaving and pitching, but never wavering from their direct course towards the beaches. Naval commanders checked their positions and glanced at their watches. With the precision of long training the first assault was launched.

**WET LANDING.** A Commando is halfway down the ramp . . . a sudden swell lifts the light assault craft . . . there is a wild struggle for balance . . . the man pitches into the sea.

In the tiny craft the men crouched up close so that they touched each other. From the 'Mason Line', halfway up the Cotentin peninsula to 'Trout Line', just west of the River Orne, the craft rolled like a wave towards the West Wall.

On the left were the 3rd Division, 'Montgomery's Ironsides', beside them the Canadian 3rd Division, then the 'Geordies'—the 50th T.T. Division. To the right were the 1st and 4th U.S. Divisions.

In the vast wave of L.c.As. each man sat tensely waiting, waiting—each desperately alone. Some thought of home, some prayed, some stretched a stiff joint, checked their kit—others were just seasick and retched.

The gap to the beaches closed. Ahead the D.D. tanks looking pitifully small in the waves churned forward. In L.c.Ts. the R.E. armoured vehicles swept on ahead quickly. On the flanks

**LIFE LINE.** American infantry haul two of their comrades ashore from a wrecked craft.

**BATTLE HAZE.** The smoke from a burning tank gives cover to attacking Commandos.

of the British beaches lights flicked out. Two X-craft, midget submarines, commanded by Lieut. Honour and Lieut. Hudspeth were in position almost on the shore. They had lain on the bottom for two days waiting for the Armada to arrive. Between the invaders and the enemy, they surfaced and flashed their signals. The crews were often washed off the tiny craft . . . they struggled back on . . . the lights continued to flash.

The violent racket increased, whining, crackling, roaring, to a crescendo filling the world and turning it to hell. The defences were being finally ' drenched before the touch down.

Crouched low in the L.c.As. the men absorb the frightful noise. Shells began to burst around the craft. Some sank, the others did not check. Suddenly there was a grinding as the first craft hit the beaches. Along the front there was one order—

" Come on—OUT ! "

The 4th U.S. Division touched down a mile o ᵀ their planned position and, with th(	tide well out, had a five hundred yard dash to reach the cover of the sand dunes. The enemy were still stunned by the ferocity of the final drenching and resistance was soon cracked. In brief staccato bursts of fire the infantry blazed away as the defenders were annihilated.

A few miles east at Omaha, the most grim, bloody battle of the invasion raged. Low cloud and dust raised by the first bombardment covered the beaches. Bombers and naval gunners left a safety margin to make sure of not hitting their own troops, with the result that the beaches were untouched, the shells and bombs falling further inland. The sea was so rough that one regiment decided not to launch their D.D. tanks, the other did and most of them sank.

The leading units of the 116th U.S. Regiment touched down to unload into a murderous fire. Men were hit as they leapt out of the craft and slumped into the sea. Within minutes the leading companies were no longer a striking force, they were desperate men striving to survive.

The destroyers and smaller naval craft were magnificent, driving almost on to the beach as they blazed at the enemy strongpoints and machine gun posts. More troops came in. On the flanks progress was made and units swung round to assist their comrades.

Slowly, the beach was cleared and a move made inland. At once minefields took their toll. There were mines everywhere and as the U.S. troops had no R.E. tanks to clear them the advance was marked by lines of wounded men— men not daring to move for fear of setting off another.

**ASSAULT.** They land. Soaking, panting, cursing, groaning, men of the assault brigade gain the beach. Machine guns rattle, mortar bombs explode as sergeants regroup their platoons.

**RAMPS DOWN.** An infantryman crouches ready to dash ashore. D.D. tanks are already ashore with the R.E. armoured vehicles.

**GET IN THERE !** Clear of the inferno of the beach, assault troops move forward determinedly to fight their way to the first village.

This was the story of Omaha, the bloodiest, dourest struggle of the day.

To the east the British assault went in with cold fury and determination. Gallant tank men drove into the sea 5,000 yards off shore to swim in and hit the beach ahead of the assaulting infantry and the flails, bulldozers and armoured vehicles of the R.Es.

On the 50th Division beach the bombardment had been effective and the assault companies of the 69th and 231st Brigades tore across the bullet swept beaches while the R.E. vehicles cleared mines, made exits and silenced strongpoints.

Beside them the Canadian 7th and 8th Brigades fought with such fierce dash that within a short while there was hardly a defender left alive on the beach.

The most vital assault was the 3rd Division's on the east. They were to hold the left flank and send reinforcements to the hard pressed 6th Airborne Division on the River Orne and the Caen Canal.

Into the nightmare of H-hour the leading units hit the beach and fought fiendishly to clear the foreshore and the strongpoints in the sand dunes. Through flames . . . smoke . . . stench . . . the stutter of Spandaus . . . the clonk of mortars—the men fought, off the beaches forcing their way into the villages of Hermanville and Ouistreham

The Allied assault was in.

**INFERNO.** Shells rain on the beach . . . a vehicle explodes in flames, but craft press on in undeterred by beach obstacles and the murderous enemy gunfire.

**DRENCHING FIRE.** A rocket craft fires a salvo that equals the fire power of 200 destroyers. These craft moved right into the beaches to give support.

**S.O.S.** American survivors from a wrecked craft are rescued from a Carley float.

**BIRD'S EYE VIEW** from an Allied aircraft. The foreshore is pitted and scarred by shells and bombs while, on the beach, the heavy sea batters assault craft, pounding them against each other.

**EXTENDED ORDER.** Ahead of them shells from supporting destroyers soltens up enemy resistance, behind them enemy shells churn up the beach . . . the invaders thrust on in. Every minute a machine gun opens up from a new position . . . there is death at every step.

**GET DOWN !** There is a moment's check . . . bullets whine overhead ; on the left a man turns on his back hit in the face, the others crouch ready to advance as soon as the order is given. Close against each other every man feels infinitely vulnerable.

**DIRECT HIT.** One second a flail tank roars ashore, the next there is a pall of smoke . . . an 88 mm. shell has scored a direct hit. Many vehicles never reached the shore once the enemy guns were concentrated on the narrow strips of the assault beaches.

**PATH CLEARED.** On the sky-line a flail-tank clears a path through a minefield. Behind it Commandos move off the beach towards their objective inland. Sergeants were telling men not to bunch—a shell does less damage when the troops are well spread out.

**WELL DONE THOSE MEN !** Weighed down with 90 lbs of kit, the last men off struggle valiantly through the waves clutching ammunition boxes. Behind them the landing ship backs off, the prow battered and ramp littered.

B Y midday the beaches were practically cleared of immediate opposition except at Omaha where the 1st U.S. Division were still battling grimly for a foothold. Elsewhere along the front the inter-mediate and follow-through brigades landed almost unopposed. As they touched down Germans, shocked and weary, clambered out of trenches on to the sand, their hands raised in surrender.

The sea had not abated. Waves running at an angle to the shore lifted the small landing craft to drop them crashing down, their ramps buckled or wrenched off by the tremendous impact. Shells rained down and many craft were hit.

Laden ' like ruddy Christmas trees ' men emerged from below on to the ships' decks blinking in the sunlight, their stomachs queasy with sea-sickness.

They were deafened by the fantastic noise, which was a prelude to their first glimpse of the nightmare awaiting them. Ashore, buildings blazed, men who had not survived the first assault lay grotesquely, grey and chill. Shells and bombs churned up the sand.

The men were shocked, but not deterred. No one quavered as they clambered down the steep ramps and stepped off into the angry sea.

Off the ramps many stepped into over four feet of water, others landed almost dry. Some stumbled and clutched frantically at the rail : ramps smashed and men fell headlong into the sea.

On the beaches death reigned. The

**LIFE LINES.** At midday the sea was running high; shells and mortar bombs were still falling as the 9th Infantry Brigade landed. Here men of the Ulster Rifles wade ashore with folding bicycles. They were to thrust out of the beach head southwards to Caen.

**FIRST HAZARD.** The ramps are buckled and smashed by the heaving sea. Impatient French Commandos crouch on the stern eager to get ashore—their shore. Every second is precious. The enemy machine-gun, mortar and artillery fire make the beach a death-trap to those who hesitate.

**THE ENEMY SEA.** A haze from the inferno on the beach drifts across the craft as men, weighted with equipment, battle valiantly ashore.

**CLOSE IN.** Frantically men clear the ramps before the craft is grounded—or hit by a shell.

initial surprise over, the Germans fought back savagely, every gun trained on the shore.

" Follow me! " All along the coast platoon commanders bawled the same order as they led their men off the beach exits. At Omaha an American colonel won fame with his cry : " Two kinds of people are staying on this beach, the dead and those who are going to die— now let's get the hell out of here ".

Already Beach Groups were trying desperately to establish order, and military police worked fiendishly to get tanks and vehicles inland. The high tide had narrowed the beach to a few yards so that unless vehicles touched down opposite an exit, it was almost impossible for them to manoeuvre off.

Behind the shore many minefields were still wired off, the " ACHTUNG MINEN " signs with skull and cross-bones still in place. The surprise had been so complete, and the first wave of the assault had moved in so quickly the enemy had not had time to remove them.

Through intense shell-fire the second wave moved inland. It was chaos. Frequently the landing craft touched down, backed off, and came in again to avoid being beached. Men came ashore in small groups, many losing touch with their platoons and companies, but they were so well briefed that each man knew exactly where to assemble and how to get there. In twos and threes, sections and platoons, the units formed up into striking forces.

In this blinding nightmare of flashes, burning, smoke, violence and destruction there were few signs of civilians although at Colleville-sur-Orne the gallant Mayor came down to welcome the invaders complete in a gleaming fireman's helmet that might equally well have served for a coal scuttle . . . a postman stood at the garden gate of a villa to hand over the post to a woman —behind her the villa was just rubble.

On the left the 9th and 185th Brigades thrust in to enlarge the 3rd Division's foothold while the 1st S.S. Brigade moved speedily inland to reinforce the hard-pressed 6th Airborne Division. One unit—No. 4 Commando —branched off alone to tackle the seemingly impregnable defences round the coastal battery at Ouistreham.

Occasionally there were checks as the leading platoons came under fire from machine gunners who fought fanatically until they died behind their guns. In the hedgerows and in trees snipers claimed their victims, but the advance continued.

Next to the 3rd British Division, the Canadian 7th and 8th Brigades were fighting swiftly and violently and were held up only by the chaos behind them. When their reserve brigade, the 9th, landed at midday, the beach and streets were so cluttered up with vehicles and armour nose to tail that it was some time before any advance could be made.

On their right the veterans of the 50th Division had seven exits cleared from

**CHINS UP.** The beach shelves sharply . . . men step off the ramp into four feet of water.

**PANZERS AHEAD.** Confidently the crew of a 3rd Division carrier speed ashore towing an anti-tank gun ready to face the Panzers who are expected to counter-attack in the evening.

**RATIONS UP !** Dukws chug through the heavy sea bringing in rations, and taking out wounded to returning craft.

the shore and were able to advance rapidly despite the harassing fire that continued to pour from the strongpoint at Le Hamel. This was only stopped when, covered by naval gunfire, a two-mile thrust was made along the coast annihilating enemy strongpoints en route to take Arromanche and secure the site for the British Mulberry.

At Omaha, after the first murderous contact—for it could hardly be called an assault—the position slowly began to stabilise. As the reinforcements moved in so destroyers came up almost on to the beach to blast at the enemy. Men of the 1st U.S. Division who met the full might of the West Wall, gritted their teeth and fought back with magnificent valour to cut a bloody trail through the enemy positions towards the Colleville-St. Laurent road.

Their comrades of the 4th Division at Utah who met with much less opposition, took every advantage surprise had given them and the follow-up units were swiftly unloaded into the bridge-head. By midday they had linked up with the parachutists who, having landed in the early hours of the morning, had already thrown the enemy into disorder and gained firm footholds.

In the evening the Americans consolidated Omaha bridgehead. Along the rest of the front the Allies were firmly ashore and thrusting through the enemy defences. The West Wall had been smashed.

**WATERPROOFED** Bren-gun carriers of the 3rd Canadian Division plunge off the ramp of a tank landing craft and struggle on to the beach already clear of mined obstacles.

**BEACH BARRAGE.** Shells and mortar bombs turn the beach into a blazing bedlam. The man in the foreground is wounded, others take shelter behind a Churchill tank waiting for the barrage to lift before getting clear of the beach and moving off to assembly areas.

**LITTLE SHIPS.** Looking like tadpoles from an Allied aircraft, the tiny assault craft dash busily to and from the beach. On D-Day over 5,000 ships and craft were involved in the initial assault operation.

**HOT SPOT.** Smoke from an exploding shell drifts up behind a jeep. Men who must stay on the beach dig—dig for their lives in the soft sand.

**DRYSHOD—ALMOST.** American infantry get a comparatively dry landing as they go in to support the now tiring first assault troops in the bridgehead.

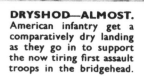

**THRUSTING IN.** There is determination in every step as Commandos march off the beach towards their first objective inland.

**MOBILE INVADERS.** A carrier crew search a shattered villa as laden assault troops wheel their 'airborne' bicycles off the shore to fight towards Caen. The bicycles were of little use. The resistance was so stubborn, riding them was like being a sitting partridge.

**ROAD CLEAR.** Past buildings shattered by the initial 'drenching' of the shore, the slow move inland continues.

# BEACHES CLEARED

**FOR THEM IT'S OVER.** The invaders are thrusting inland : on the beach ragged, bewildered Germans are rounded up. They had endured the full might of the allied assault. They are alive but captive.

**THE PRICE.** Only when the day was late and the invaders had carried the battle inland was the cost reckoned. Assault craft lay idly drifting with the tide, wrecked by mines and shell-fire, whilst the beach was strewn with battered gear. The sea caressed the fallen.

THE afternoon wore on and the sounds of gunfire receded as the assault troops fought their way violently inland. Even at Omaha where the enemy had put up the bitterest resistance, the gallant American 1st Division had secured a foothold and fought magnificently.

Back on the beaches there was a momentary lull. For a brief time the din and clamour had passed ; little was left but destruction.

Waves lapped against battered tanks and vehicles that were already waterlogged, seemingly useless. Covered with sand and seaweed they looked already as though they had lain there for a long time. Bicycles, respirators and kit of all sorts were strewn on the sand. Wrecked landing craft lay deserted on the foreshore, some high and dry on the beach, others rocking idly in the tide their hulls holed where they had been driven relentlessly through the beach obstacles until blasted by mines. Still more showed the ragged scars where they had been hit by 88 mm. shells.

Men who that morning had hurled themselves gallantly against the might of the great West Wall lay where they had fallen. Their valour will shine through history : they came first, they stayed last.

This then was the aftermath. This was the price.

But there was no time to wonder, no time to grieve. The beaches had to be cleared. Frogmen and highly trained specialists of the Navy's Obstruction Clearance Units were already at work dealing with the underwater defences.

Shells fell intermittently as Naval Beachmasters, many of whom had learnt their tasks in other landings at Sicily, Salerno and Anzio, took charge of landing arrangements and prepared for the next wave of eight ship convoys due to arrive the following day.

Salvage officers inspected the damaged craft. The Beach Groups, which had landed with the first assaults, were in operation.

To the Royal Engineers fell the dangerous task of finding and disarming the mines. Tracks had to be laid for heavy vehicles and tanks, and new exits cleared from the beaches. With the sappers, the Pioneers sweated and strained.

Moving cautiously along the verge of the shore a sapper checked suddenly in his stride, almost on top of a mine.

"Whew," he gasped, "I nearly missed that one."

The sergeant looked over. "You wouldn't have," he said grimly. "Take it steady."

The work went on with death as the foreman.

Bulldozers cleared wreckage and made level tracks. Military police erected signposts, and directed traffic towards

. . . FOREVER ENGLAND. Beneath a battered German strongpoint on a French beach they fell. They had made history and paid the price that it should not be repeated.

DIRECT HIT. Despite being torpedoed just forward of the bridge L.c.T. 921 managed to get back to the calm of Southampton Water. Her crew were posted : her job was done.

CLOSE SUPPORT. Hard after the infantry, Sherman tanks grind off the now cleared beach towards the exits. In less than an hour they will be in action against the Panzers.

**ATLANTIC WALL.** The Tellermines that were attached to them disarmed, beach obstacles are piled clear of the waterline to give landing craft a clear, safe run in to the beach. By the evening of D-Day, the West Wall's first line of defence is just a pile of scrap.

**THE YANKS ARE COMING.** Beneath the shell of a shattered German strongpoint U.S. infantry struggle ashore laden with their kit. There is no resistance, the beach is cleared.

the battle that raged two miles inland.

Slowly order came from chaos—order dispelled occasionally as a shell created havoc, casualties, and, to the Beach Groups, more work.

Meanwhile the dead were buried with reverence, and the wounded had to be attended. Those lying on the beach were carried into shelter while, back from the front, came a continuous stream, some walking, some on stretchers—British, Americans, Germans; all simply 'wounded' to the men of the Red Cross.

The R.A.M.C. surgeons and orderlies had worked unceasingly almost from the moment the first waves touched down. Now, some hours after, marquees were pitched beneath trees and operating theatres set up. Men racked and sweating with pain were eased with morphia. Once treated they were loaded into every available craft going back to England, the serious cases being carried in stretchers to R.A.S.C. Dukws which ferried them out to hospital ships and L.c.Ts.

Undaunted by the chaos of immobile vehicles, R.A.O.C. and R.E.M.E. craftsmen set to work to recover those that could still be made serviceable. Linesmen of the U.S. Army and the Royal Signals toiled over their lines and connected field telephones to ensure the passage of vital orders.

As they worked they were protected by units of famous regiments—the Berkshires, the Kings, Borderers and the

Bedfords. It was a bridgehead within a bridgehead.

The men worked, sweated, ' brewed up ', paused to time the whine of a shell before getting down—already they were veterans.

Soon there were small groups of prisoners. Gaunt, ragged men, their nerves shattered by the almighty pounding of the initial assault. They stood aimlessly, hopelessly, some afraid, others trying to retain their dignity. Gazing out to sea they saw the vast mass of Allied shipping lying off the shore and knew this was defeat.

No one doubted what the night would bring and the R.A.F. and U.S. units hoisted barrage balloons along the beach while gunners manhandled Ack-Ack guns into position. Only in darkness would the enemy challenge the Allied superiority in the air.

Houses that had earlier been set ablaze by the naval bombardment now smouldered. There was a reek of charred embers mingled with the tang of high explosives. But the fire had passed, already the work of reconstruction had begun.

**THE DEFEATED.** In the British sector the first prisoners wait to be directed to a P.O.W. cage. Some are defiant, others submissive—they know that this is the beginning of the end of the Nazi domination of Europe.

**FLOTSAM.** A wrecked tank, its gun still pointed towards the enemy, stands deserted. Its job is done, the assault troops are firmly established and now, beside it, a Somerfeld track has been laid down to enable the follow-up armoured brigade to get inland swiftly.

**BRIDGEHEAD.** A mile inland the battle rages fiercely. On the beach sappers, pioneers, military police and the Beach Groups waste no time starting to clear up ready for reinforcements to arrive.

**SPECIAL DESPATCH.** Three hours after the assault first went in, a war correspondent interviews R.N. Commandos beside a wrecked landing craft high on the beach at La Riviere.

**STRANDED.** High and dry L.s.Ts. unload direct on to the shore where U.S. engineers have laid tracks.

**10 MINUTE SMOKE.** Commodore Douglas-Pennant, commander of ' G ' Force chats to R.M. Commandos who have been clearing beach obstacles. Already their first task is done, landing craft can land safely without any danger from mined obstacles.

**EVEN DIGNITY IS GONE.** Wretched, tired, their nerves almost shattered by the appalling fury of the Allied assault, Germans stand in the sea warming their hands after fixing a tow to a jeep. Behind them is a flail tank used to clear paths through minefields.

**NEW TENANTS.** Trenches held only hours before by Germans are reinforced for protection against the continual shelling and mortar fire. (*Left*) A jar of naval rum washed up on the beach gives new heart to the hard-working men of a beach clearance group.

**CLOSE UP.** Lieut. Commander Hans Hamilton and Major Clayton, R.E. examine the Tellermine attached to a beach obstacle.

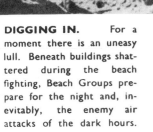

**DIGGING IN.** For a moment there is an uneasy lull. Beneath buildings shattered during the beach fighting, Beach Groups prepare for the night and, inevitably, the enemy air attacks of the dark hours.

**THUMBS UP.** Hours ago the 'Hindenburg Bastion' was one of the major strong-points of the West Wall. Now, with a little alteration to the original German title, it houses the crew of an advance British Bofors gun.

HINDENBURG

UNDER NEW MANAGEMENT

SGT. SAVAGE

AND HIS CHINDITS

# AIRBORNE ASSAULT

**AIRBORNE ARMADA.** The air landing brigade fly over the Channel to support their comrades of the 6th Airborne Division fighting on the banks of the River Orne. Our air superiority was so great the gliders flew in without being molested by the Luftwaffe.

**COMBINED OPS.** Night approaches as the gliders fly low over the bombarding ships.

THE most wondrous and splendid spectacle of D-Day came late in the warm sunny evening.

Men who that morning had felt the exhilaration of the first victory on the beaches were tiring, yet mentally they were tensed waiting for the expected counter-attack from the 12th S.S. Hitler Youth and 21st Panzer Divisions.

Suddenly someone gasped : " Cor blimey — look ! "

As they gazed up over their shoulders the men's eyes brightened, their hearts throbbed warm. The sky seemed filled with aircraft as gracefully, majestically, two hundred and fifty gliders sailed in. Over the coast the planes cast off and turned back towards England : for a second each glider seemed to poise then, swiftly and silently, dived down into the bridgehead.

The 6th Air Landing Brigade had come in to reinforce the hard pressed 6th Airborne Division on the left flank.

No Luftwaffe planes had attempted to intercept ; the R.A.F. tug planes seemed to disdain the flak that burst around them. It was simply a superb manifestation of the complete Allied domination in the air over the front.

In a few minutes it was all over. The gliders were down, the planes back over the horizon; yet every man in the bridgehead felt a warm glow of pride mingled with reassurance.

But it was east of the Orne where they touched down that the gliders were most welcome. There the paratroops and advance gliders had already been in action for some twenty hours fighting desperately against increasing odds to hold the vital bridges over the Orne and the Caen Canal.

They were the spearhead of the invasion. Of them there are no pictures : they came in darkness. There is only the story, a story of courage and heroism that was unsurpassed in this day when bravery was commonplace.

. . .

The battle for the bridges began just after midnight.

Still far out in the Channel, the invasion Armada was steaming steadily towards Normandy when the first six gliders slipped their tow ropes and sped down towards their objectives, the only sound being the sigh of the wind whistling past their wings.

**WELCOME.** Assault troops of the 3rd Div. are cheered as paratroops drop to fight beside them.

**CAST OFF.** As the towing planes wheel back towards the coast, gliders crash land well behind the enemy lines, the men ready for action.

**ALLIED AID.** American Flying Forts drop guns and ammunition to men of the Maquis who were warned of the Invasion by the B.B.C.

**ON TARGET.** Supplies, ordered by wireless, drop on 6th Airborne Division positions which hold the left flank of the bridgehead.

At the canal three gliders crash landed almost on the bridge itself. The men leapt out frantically into bedlam as the enemy opened up with Spandaus and rifles. Scorning the fire the 'Red Devils' hurled themselves on the enemy positions and, in a matter of minutes, the first small, vital battle of the invasion was fought and won.

Nearby the men bound for the Orne bridge touched down some way from their objective. Crashing out of their wrecked gliders they moved forward without a pause ready for action : but there was none—the enemy had fled.

Both bridges had been taken intact.

In the meantime the pathfinders had marked out the dropping zones and over two thousand paratroops came in. It was a difficult drop, many having to jump from weaving aircraft with a 60 lb. kitbag tied to one leg.

In the wilderness of the night men were slow to rally. Due to launch a battalion attack against the strongly held Merville battery, which could threaten the seaborne assault, the Commanding Officer of the 9th Parachute Battalion found he had only 150 men—but the attack went in and after a desperate bloody battle lasting over an hour the position was taken, a success signal fired, and a carrier pigeon despatched with the news.

Before the dawn of D-Day General Gale's 6th Airborne Division were in position and holding the enemy.

Meanwhile to the west the 82nd and 101st U.S. Airborne Divisions had landed on the neck of the Cotentin peninsula. Running into flak the pilots of the aircraft flew too fast and too high making the jumping exceedingly difficult, men being scattered over a wide area. The 101st Division were particularly badly scattered and of over 6,000 parachutists, only 1,000 had reached their rendezvous by dawn.

The 82nd Division took Ste. Mere Eglise to block the Carentan-Cherbourg road, but elsewhere in the dropping zone the paratroops were so heavily engaged fighting for their lives they had no chance of performing their operational tasks of blowing the bridges over the River Douve, or forming a compact bridgehead over the Merderet.

Never was night so long as, fighting valiantly, the Allied Airborne forces held off all attacks and waited for the seaborne troops to land with the dawn. Only then could they expect reinforcements.

**HOLD TIGHT !** Silently, gliders full of troops armed to the teeth swoop down to land in a wheat-field on the evening of D-Day.

**LITTER OF WAR.** Horsa gliders, their fuselages detached for quick unloading lie deserted in fields north-east of Caen.

**HEDGED IN.** Seen from an Allied aircraft, dozens of gliders lay within yards of each other, a testimony to the skill of the Army glider pilots who had landed them according to plan.

**EXPENDED.** A stiff breeze drags the parachutes across the dropping zone—there was no time to collect them, every second was precious in the dash to capture the vital bridges over the River Orne and the Caen Canal. The glider below crash landed on the banks of the Canal.

**ON OBJECTIVE.** The first battle is over and the left flank is secure. On the field telephone a signaller reports " All correct, sir."

**CONSOLIDATION.** Commandos, who have fought their way from the beaches to link up with the 6th Airborne Division units, dig in.

**RECCE.** Paratroops probe a shattered village with, left, a member of the Maquis. In the foreground lies a German, his last battle over.

**IN AND OUT.** Weary American glider pilots who have fought their way back through the enemy lines to the beaches return to England by water to fly back more reinforcements.

**FIRST BACK.** Lieut. General Browning, G.O.C. Airborne Forces was Transport Command's first passenger to be flown back to England. Battle commander of the 6th Airborne Division was General Gale.

# BASH ON!

**COMBINED ASSAULT.** Off the beach a D.D. tank roars into the attack. Infantry, moving at the double despite their heavy loads, keep close to get protection from small arms fire. The first crust of the West Wall smashed, the liberating armies bash on.

THE landings had been made and the West Wall breached. As the day wore on towards evening there was a sense of anti-climax. From the tense desperation of the morning came reaction. Men laughed easily, they were elated, supremely confident—they "hadn't half shaken the bloody Jerries".

No man doubted they were there to stay but, the supreme effort of the first assault over, it was hard to keep up the speed of the attack.

From the first violent assault, the attack had slowed to walking pace by the evening of D-Day.

Behind Caen, Rommel issued orders for the counter-attack. Infantry were to seal off the Americans while the 21st Panzers and the 12th S.S. struck at the British.

Meyer, commander of the 12th S.S. was bursting with confidence, scorning the British as "little fish" that his troops, the elite of the Hitler Youth, would throw back into the sea.

**"MOVING UP NOW—OVER."** So the messages flash back over the R/T as tanks advance.

**ATTACK.** Any moment all hell may break loose as the hidden enemy open fire and bring down an artillery barrage on an S.O.S. line. But steadily 3rd Div. infantry advance towards Caen.

**POINT DUTY.** Military police keep the column moving through a consolidation area, while riflemen give their rifles a pull-through.

During the afternoon twenty-four Panzer tanks had thrust in between the British and Canadian bridgeheads, but they were beaten off by tanks and anti-tank guns to withdraw leaving five behind, smouldering wrecks. A major Panzer attack planned for the evening was still-born when the air landing brigade swept over the bridgehead.

The Allies gained first prizes of the invasion. A major of the Durham Light Infantry drove triumphantly to his Company H.Q., in a captured 10 h.p. car. A truck carrying thousands of francs was seized—the pay of a whole company ; another was loaded with hot soup, coffee and fresh bread for a forward German unit . . . a platoon commander looked back goggle-eyed as his runner followed him out of a captured German strongpoint puffing a huge cigar and with a bottle of wine tied to his waist. The enemy had done themselves well—he was glad to say.

The long evening wore on to a night little different from the day except there was less light. It was just a halt with the enemy often less than two hundred yards ahead. There was no sleep. Listening posts were put out and behind them men dug in while fighting patrols, their faces blackened, moved silently forward along hedgerows to strike terror in the night.

When they clashed with the enemy the night was shattered with the bursting of grenades and the rapid stutter of Sten guns. In a few seconds there was silence again, but for the moans of the wounded.

With 'stand to' came dawn, the racket of machine guns and renewed ferocity from the artillery.

At the front it was lonely, each company seemed so pitifully small against the backcloth of the unending noise and mighty pounding of guns. Then the tanks moved up and the infantry was reassured. Sometimes there were mistakes.

In the van of the 3rd Division the Ulster Rifles were moving up the edge of a copse when a hail of tracer came at them from some of their own supporting tanks. For a few minutes there was chaos, but little damage was done. Next day the tanks repaid in full.

Supporting the Ulsters in an attack on Cambes Wood the tanks stayed with the riflemen as they advanced through what seemed an impassable enemy barrage. With them were five R.E. armoured vehicles which came to grips with the enemy and fought until they were all knocked out.

To the right the Canadians fought forward magnificently and threatened to outflank Caen and take the airfield at Carpiquet. Only after suffering very

'WARE SNIPERS. In the open the invaders move fast—every window may hide a sniper.

EYES OF THE NAVY. Observers for supporting naval guns lay cable as they move up.

THE INNOCENT. Gentle cows, now dead, bloated and stinking, lie in almost every field of the bullet-swept battle area inland from the beachhead.

FOLLOW THROUGH. Assault troops get a brief rest as reserve units, fresh from the beach, come up to sustain the attack.

**ARMOUR ADVANCES.** Over dusty tracks—to leave the roads clear for infantry—tanks move up swiftly, their path having already been cleared through the minefields by flail tanks.

**DIRECT HIT.** The flash is blinding, the violent roar of the explosion echoes across the fields . . . a German mortar has scored a direct hit on an ammunition lorry. Undamaged, the tanks press the attack home.

heavy casualties did Meyer's S.S. troopers stem the advance—the " little fish " were not so little.

From Omaha and Utah beachheads the Americans made rapid progress across the Cotentin peninsula, linking up with their airborne forces and fighting from hedgerow to hedgerow.

Squadrons of tanks moved up, the distorted metallic voices from the R/T sets echoing over the thunder of the tracks and engines. The infantry, heads bent forward beneath the weight of their kit, trudged on in single file, each man a walking arsenal. They were oblivious of the vehicles that trundled past covering them with dust and smoke. When they halted for a few minutes packs were eased off and the black, sweat-stained patches of their battle-dress blouses steamed in the June sun. A whistle blew and they heaved to their feet, desperately weary yet never thinking of stopping. The infantry bashed on. . . .

**THE HARD WAY.** Infantry, every man carrying all he needs to fight—and live, trudge past tanks which cleared the way.

**DEAR MUM . . .** In a tank harbour, the crew write their first letters home—or, exhausted, curl up and go to sleep.

**CHECK.** Ahead, the leading platoon deals with a machine gun nest. Behind, men wait, ready to meet any attack from the flanks.

**STRETCHER CASE.** On a board between two rifles, Commandos carry their wounded Company Sergeant Major back to a forward Field Dressing Station.

**GOOD PATIENT.** Jasper, a Labrador who hunts mines, has a wounded ear gently treated by Sergeant Ridgeway, R.A.V.C.

**LAST STAND.** There was a sharp violent battle ; a tank is knocked out ; a Panzer grenadier lies dead. The invaders move up and take the position. Another small part of France has been liberated.

**STUNNED** by the violent battle raging round them, groups of villagers watch tanks roar through La Delivrande. (*Inset right*) An aged patriot unfurls long-folded Allied flags.

**CHANGING FORTUNES.** In groups in doorways, villagers watch impassive prisoners marching back. For four long years they have endured German occupation, now they can think, act and talk freely again. Yet there is no joy, no sorrow—they just stare.

**BRIEFING.** Captain J. F. Burgess puts his party in the picture before they move to their observation post. It was he who directed the fire of H.M.S. *Ramilles* which had devastating effect on strongpoints in the early stages.

**MINE CLEARANCE.** Amid the ruins of the village of Tilly-sur-Seulles, Royal Engineers sweep the main street with mine detectors while riflemen search the wrecked buildings for snipers.

**ALL ABOARD.** A forward infantry carrier moves up giving a lift to men in motley kit. They're efficient, confident and, already veterans. They were the spearhead of the British 3rd Division in the early thrust towards Caen.

**BAYEUX IS FREE !** On a makeshift platform Allied officers receive bouquets. It is D plus 3, a day Bayeux will never forget— nor yet the day De Gaulle arrives in France. Men shake his hand, women blink back tears—after four years they are free from occupation.

**VICTORY PARADE.** Grimy, exhausted, but victorious, the crew of a Canadian carrier trundle back from the front with, behind them, a column of battle-worn German prisoners.

"SOME CHICKEN". It is only D plus 6 when Mr. Churchill arrives in the beachhead to be met by General Montgomery. As the Dukw arrives the enemy are only four miles away. Some neck!

# Good Old Winnie!

"WISH YOU WERE HERE", wrote Mr. Churchill to President Roosevelt after his visit to the beaches. The Prime Minister stands on the landing craft as it heads in towards the Normandy shore.

**AIRCRAFT OVERHEAD.** Mr. Churchill, complete with his well-known cigar, watches a flight of Allied aircraft flying over the beach-head and inland to attack enemy concentrations. With him are General O'Connor, Field Marshal Smuts, General Montgomery and General Alanbrooke.

# FRONT LINE AIRSTRIP

**STERN CRITICS.** The ground crew sit watching critically as a rocket-firing Typhoon takes off in a cloud of dust from an airstrip.

**SIGNALS AHEAD.** Passing through a village an R.A.F. signals truck leads a carrier of the 50th T.T. Division—the assault troops. Work on the airstrips was commenced right on D-Day.

**STERN CRITICS.** The ground crew sit watching critically as a rocket-firing Typhoon takes off in a cloud of dust from an airstrip.

A HUNDRED AND FIFTY yards from the enemy a Canadian infantryman whipped the magazine from his Bren. The barrel was hot so he paused to look up as a Spitfire circled almost casually overhead. Suddenly its undercarriage appeared.

"Gosh," he muttered to his No. 2. "I believe that guy's gonna land!"

The Spitfire disappeared behind some trees and touched down.

On D plus 3, for the first time since 1940, Allied air forces were operating from France.

Within three weeks thirty squadrons had bases in the beachhead.

Long before D-Day the assault area had been carefully studied from the air and sites selected for airstrips, and, as soon as the invading infantry had secured a foothold, Sappers and Pioneers moved up.

Work started as the battle raged not half a mile forward. Shells whined overhead, Spandaus stuttered, but the airfield construction companies 'got cracking' despite them.

The strip was marked out, bulldozers levelled it. To keep down dust which might do damage to an aircraft

**MANY HANDS** make light work of laying the wire mesh for a new airstrip. The essence is speed—speed to enable fighters to operate and give the advancing troops close support.

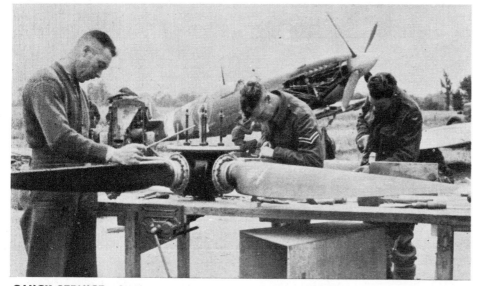

**QUICK SERVICE.** On the edge of a cornfield the 'carpenters' shop' work on an airscrew. The time for servicing an aircraft is cut down to a bare minimum, but still the job is well done.

engine, hessian was laid down, then wire mesh—hundreds of tons of it. Grass seed was planted and water was pumped up.

R.A.F. ground crews set up workshops in corn fields and under the trees. Rockets and cannon shells were brought up to rearm the planes. Refuelling vehicles arrived ; each one a death trap if hit by a shell—the drivers had guts.

As Sappers and Pioneers worked, others kept watch for enemy aircraft and 'timed' the whine of shells as they came over. There was ' all round defence '—at least it was planned that there should at least be some warning of an enemy attack.

.    .    .

Having blasted away an obstacle on the airstrip, two sappers looked to see four Germans not twenty yards away from them.

They dived frantically for their rifles, but there was no need, the Germans held their hands high in surrender. They had had enough.

Edgy and doubtful one sapper searched the prisoners while the other kept them covered.

An hour later the Germans were voluntarily unloading R.A.F. equipment—little more than a mile from their own lines.

.    .    .

The Allied planes tackled everything : laying down barrages, softening up enemy positions, supporting infantry and tank attacks, and constantly straffing and bombing enemy troops and lines of communication. German counter attacks were wrecked by our planes even before they reached the start line.

Day in and day out the pilots took off within range of the enemy guns. More squadrons came in to the beachhead. Tents appeared round the airstrips although tired pilots more often took rest in slit trenches, the only defence against mortaring and shelling.

The ground crews worked like fiends to keep every aircraft serviceable.

" Blimey, a Brylcreem boy," became an ejaculation couched in respect from the armies.

Tens of thousands of sorties were flown over Normandy by Allied pilots —Americans, British, Poles, Czechs and Norwegians.

One pilot, Squadron Leader Williamson, was hit by flak when bombing Villers Bocage in a Lancaster and made an emergency landing on a fighter strip only a short distance from

**PUTTING IN THE STING.** As soon as a plane reaches the dispersal point the ground crew check it over and rearm the guns. In minutes the plane is ready for take-off.

**PRANGED.** Men of the Repair and Salvage Unit literally put their backs into it to get a damaged Spitfire back into operation again.

the front. He met the forward infantry and, with dozens of offers of a ' brew up ', got personal thanks for his help from the men attacking the village . . . " you certainly shook the bastards ! "

Orders were constantly coming through . . . " Attack enemy concentration map reference 26731014". Within minutes pilots scrambled into their aircraft and were diving on the target.

In half-an-hour it was just another " wizard prang " but, to the ground troops it was another battle half won.

As the troops advanced and captured towns and villages they frequently found they were already ' occupied ' by the R.A.F. Pilots who had been forced to bale out over the enemy lines were hidden by French patriots and reappeared to welcome the advancing infantry as the enemy retreated.

It was the complete domination of the air by the Allied air forces which was the vital and, perhaps, the deciding factor in the Normandy battle.

**GROUNDED.** Captured air and ground crews of the Luftwaffe march past an Allied airstrip on their way to the beaches and a P.O.W. cage. Amongst them are Poles, Czechs and one or two German naval personnel all of whom had been brought up to attempt to hold the invaders.

**DANGER—MEN AT WORK.** While sappers and Pioneers work feverishly to complete a new runway, men watch for signs of enemy aircraft, and also for Allied aircraft wanting to come in and land

**ONE LESS.** Close behind the front R.A.F. personnel inspect the tangled wreckage of a German M.E. 109 shot down by Allied fighters. (*Left*) L.A.C. Blackett of Barnsley strips right off to get down to the job.

**FIGHTER SWEEP.** Pilots of the Royal Norwegian Air Force sweep in to attack enemy positions over the bridgehead.

**ANYTHING ELSE?** After sorties over the enemy lines an R.A.F. and a Canadian pilot report to the interrogation officer in his open air headquarters, set up in an orchard adjoining the make-shift airstrip.

**PAY PARADE.** Men of an R.A.F. beach squadron get their first pay parade in France. The pay table is a captured German beetle tank, the chair from a battered and deserted house—no one thinks it odd.

**DUSK PATROL.** Revving up ready to taxi to the runway, Allied pilots know that only at dusk will enemy aircraft dare to challenge the Allied air superiority and attack the beaches.

**SCRAMBLE.** The pilot was in readiness when the order came through . . . he dashes to his Typhoon . . . within minutes he will be airborne, a deadly answer to the menace of the Luftwaffe.

**TOP SCORER.** Wing Commander Johnny Johnson, one of the top-scoring R.A.F. pilots on the wing of his Spitfire with his Labrador, Sally, during a break between "ops." He commanded a Canadian Spitfire wing operating in the beachhead soon after the first assault.

**DISTINGUISHED VISITOR.** Ace fighter pilot, Group Captain ' Sailor ' Malan talks over the latest show with Wing Commander Compton and, in the background, a French pilot. Each day thousands of sorties were flown over Normandy giving fighter cover, straffing enemy concentrations and doing valuable reconnaissance work for General Montgomery's operational headquarters.

**WIZARD PRANG.** Behind Caen lies the graveyard of Rommel's Panzer Divisions. Often before they are able to reach the front they are targets for R.A.F. rockets—then they go no further. After the Allied break-through thousands of vehicles were found wrecked.

# MULBERRY

*The story of the harbours, each the size of Gibraltar, which were towed over to supply the invading armies.*

**CLOSE STATION.** Bow to stern, a line of blockships sunk off Arromanche lies steady in the tide.

Admiral Tennant, commander of the Mulberry operations, visits the harbour with Captain Petrie, right, who directed the actual building of the ports.

IN the courageous but tragic raid on Dieppe in 1942, the Canadians lost three-quarters of their force of 5,000 : the enemy losses had been less than 600.

These were the odds against taking a channel port—or even worse, for since that time the Germans had intensified their harbour fortifications and disposed their forces to counter any attack made on them. They were confident that, without a Channel port, the Allies could not maintain an invading army in France.

They were right—to a point. But they had not reckoned with the imaginative genius of Churchill, Mountbatten and Commodore Hughes Hallet who proposed prefabricating harbours, towing them over in sections, and set-

ting them up off the assault beaches. This plan was adopted and given the code name 'Mulberry'.

This was no story of heroics and glory, rather was it the story of British inventive genius, brilliant organization, sheer hard work in the docks, completed by the solid efficiency of the Navy.

The harbours consisted of outer floating breakwaters, inner fixed breakwaters made of concrete caissons, and floating piers running from the pierheads to the shore. Complementary to the 'Mulberries' were 'Gooseberry' harbours which were blockships sunk in lines to provide protection to the innumerable small craft immediately after D-Day before the Mulberries were properly laid and in operation.

In eight months the ports were made —vast concrete caissons, seven miles of pier roadway, and the sixty blockships for the 'Gooseberries' were prepared.

By D-Day all was set and Admiral Tennant had a force of over 15,000 men to tow the harbours over, 'plant', and maintain them.

This was a major naval operation and the greatest task ever undertaken by tugs.

With D-Day the job began. The gallant little tugs battled against mounting seas towing vast masses of 'floating ironmongery' behind them. By D plus 2 the blockships were in position and the 'Gooseberry' harbours were operating. The placing of the million and a half tons of gear for the 'Mulberries' was under way and by D plus 13 the major work was done.

Already the build-up was in progress and flat-bottomed coasters came right in to the beaches inside the shelter of the Mulberries to unload into busy Dukws. Along the causeways from the pierheads rolled an unending stream of all types of vehicles.

Then came the most violent June storm for 40 years which completely wrecked the American 'Mulberry' off St. Laurent and gravely damaged the more carefully laid British port at Arromanche. This was a bitter blow, but as soon as the storm had blown itself out parts of the American 'Mulberry' were salvaged to rebuild that at Arromanche and soon the port was back in full swing and laden convoys arrived.

The armies' supply lines were safe, despite the fact that no Channel port had been taken.

**ONE DOWN.** The first of the blockships, the S.S. *Alymare*, settles on the sea bed. Sixty ships were sunk in order to give some five and a half miles of breakwater for the two harbours.

**SHORE VIEW.** Pontoons carrying a roadway stretch from the shore to the 'spud pierheads' where vessels unload. Beyond the blockships give protection.

**THE SEA STRIKES.** The pontoons crash and tilt, the beach is littered with wreckage. This is D plus 13 when a storm almost smashed the harbours.

**FLOATING ROAD.** On pontoons the causeway is towed back into position from the pierhead to the shore. Soon vehicles will drive over them again.

**LAST LAP.** Getting the block-ships into position was a brilliant feat of seamanship. One ship out of position would have allowed the sea to surge through and greatly weaken the usefulness of the others. Despite all shore 'marks' being blown away or hidden under the pall of battle, all ships were safely placed in position by D plus 2.

**CHAR UP!** With an assortment of cups and mugs, 'matelots' crouch round the galley hatch for a cup of tea. They had a slow, dangerous trip over and now, manœuvring the harbour into position they are a sitting target for the German gunners inshore.

**DRYING OUT.** Safe inside the harbour, coasters lie high and dry at low tide and unload their cargoes into Dukws manned by drivers of the R.A.S.C.

**SUPPLY LINE.** Along roads blasted by R.Es. the Dukws carry stores direct to dumps a mile inshore.

**BLAST.** Reinforced concrete of the West Wall is blown away to make way for another road to hasten the transport of supplies from the Mulberries.

**THE SEA IS TAMED.** A rough sea runs against the blockships and caissons while, inside, the water is smooth and craft unload quickly on to the pierheads. Pontoon causeways, along which transport can travel, run direct to the shore at the top of the picture.

# BUILD-UP

**FAST WORK.** It is still D-Day but already Canadian sappers have laid tracks and, alongside the infantry, tanks roll into the bridgehead and on inland.

**DESERT RATS.** The 51st Highland Division land. No longer is it the sand of the desert, but the enemy facing them is still the same—Rommel.

THE Allied assault troops landed carrying ration packs for 48 hours, the ammunition the men carried ashore had to last them for the same period. The troops—well, there were casualties; reinforcements would be needed.

Even as the assault brigades fought their way off the beach area, Beach Groups began to operate and, despite all enemy attempts to stop them, still the huge laden convoys ploughed across the Channel.

More troops came ashore, more tanks, trucks, armoured cars. Untiring Dukws bounced through the waves on to the beach piled high with food and ammunition. Store dumps appeared.

On D-Day over thirty U-boats put to sea to attack, but Coastal Command aircraft and the Allied Navies were ready. Within a few days twelve were sunk or badly damaged and the remainder put back to port, whipped from the seas.

Air Force units on the beaches put up barrage balloons, naval officers kept tally of the craft coming in; the beachmasters' Aldis lamps clacked-clacked their signals to control the steady flow.

When the Rhino ferries proved unseaworthy in heavy weather L.s.Ts. had to discharge direct on to the beaches becoming sitting targets for six hours until the next high tide refloated them.

Time, time, time. Every hour, every minute, was invaluable.

. . .

The ramp of an L.c.T. is lowered and a truck rolls down wallowing up to the bonnet in the waves. The engine stalls and the truck blocks the way.

"Cor, if it wasn't where it is I'd swear it was a woman driver," comes a derisive yell then, impatiently, "Come on . . . get the bloody thing out of it!"

A bulldozer is already passing a tow. There is a strain, the truck lurches and is pulled ashore. The unloading continues.

. . .

Shelled and bombed day and night, the Beach Groups worked heroically and in the first six days over 300,000 men, 54,000 vehicles, and 104,000 tons of stores were unloaded.

The gap between the sea at high tide and the top of the beach was narrow —two broken-down trucks could hold up an armoured regiment. It was now that the Pioneers showed their metal.

They were not all young men, not all over-fit; theirs was the quality of rugged endurance. They cleared wreckage, found concrete mixers and built roads. Heaving, lifting, and straining they worked. Trickles of salt sweat stung their eyes only to be brushed

**HIGH TIDE.** A tank landing craft discharges directly on a difficult portion of the beach. The strip between the sea and the hinterland is narrow leaving little room for the tank to manoeuvre.

**A LIFT ASHORE.** The giant bows of a tank landing craft yawn open as American troops and vehicles unload on to a Rhino ferry for the last lap. In heavy seas the Rhinos proved unseaworthy.

**GOING HOME.** There's a long dour fight ahead of them but, checking their kit after unloading, Dutch troops are anxious to thrust northwards with the attacking armies to Holland—and home.

**ACTION AHEAD.** Perched on every available viewpoint, American follow-up troops get their first view of the battered beaches on D plus 2. *(Left)* A bulldozer chugs ashore through the waves.

away impatiently by a brawny forearm.

It was back-breaking, endless, heart-breaking work. They won no honours —only undying admiration.

No less were the efforts of the U.S. transport men, and the R.Es., the R.E.M.E., R.A.O.C. and the R.A.S.C.

It is June 16, an R.A.S.C. driver leaps out of his Dukw on to the sand. "Soaked to the ruddy skin," he curses. Looking up he is shocked to silence. General Montgomery stands talking to H.M. the King twenty yards away !

The driver feels a tingle of pride. He forgets he is wet.

• • •

The Merchant Navy scorned the enemy guns as they ran their ships right in to the shore. Typical was the courage of 63-year-old James Craigie, master of a ship bringing in over 700 tons of ammunition.

His ship was hit and abandoned but as soon as the shelling let up, the crew and R.E. stevedores reboarded her and set about unloading. Only when the shelling started again and the ship had

**LONG SHOT.** Protected by barrage balloons from raiding enemy aircraft, convoys begin to unload on the American sector of the beachhead which was still under fire from enemy guns when this picture was taken by a cameraman of the Ninth American Air Force.

been hit six times did James Craigie leave—after the crew were clear.

Convoy after convoy crossed the Channel—then came the blow.

Throughout the early stages the weather had been vile. On June 19 it was hell. A suddenly violent storm blew up, wrecked the Mulberries and, when it abated, 800 craft were stranded high and dry on the beaches.

But it was only a temporary setback.

The build up went on. Men, guns, ammunition and food poured into the bridgehead until on July 1 General Eisenhower's Chief Administrative Officer was able to report: " Commanders in the field have complete freedom of action so far as administrative arrangements are concerned."

The Navy had supplied the Army's requirements.

**ROYAL INVADER.** Only ten days after D-Day H.M. the King arrived in France. He toured the beachhead and, as Admiral Ramsay wrote then, " encouraged all British forces."

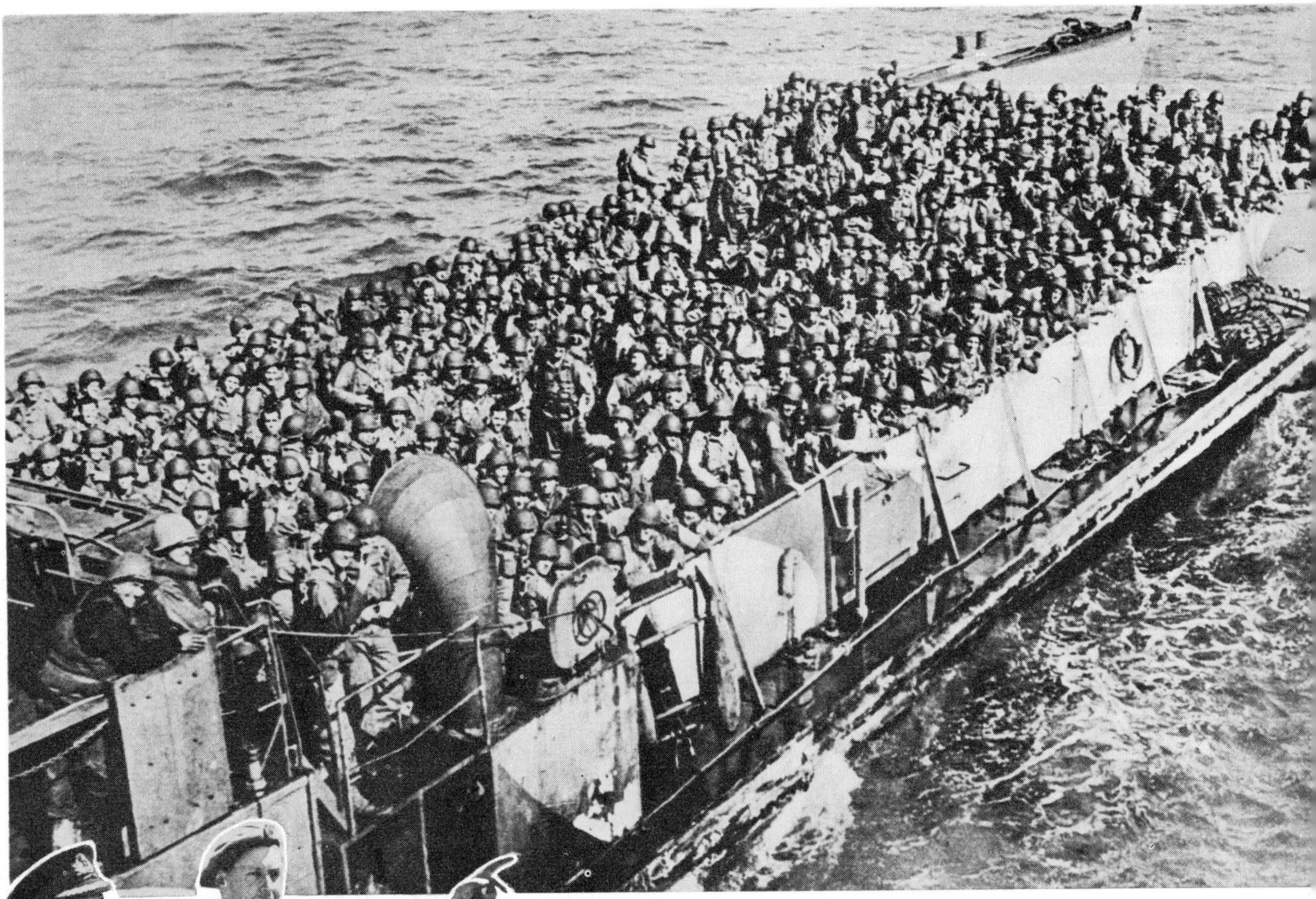

**FERRY SERVICE.** Packed tight into a tender, American troops are eager to touch down and go in to support their comrades now tiring after the first assault. (*Below* A barrage balloon bobbing low over its bow, a heavily laden Rhino ferry chugs slowly from a tank landing ship on its way to the beach where it will be swiftly unloaded

**NAVY ASHORE.**
Cmdr. A. Willmott
R.N.R., the resident
naval officer at Cour-
seulles checks details of
the unloading with an
army supplies officer.

**STAND BY.** Lying dangerously low in the heavy swell an overloaded Dukw comes alongside H.M.S. *Aristocrat* where eager hands tumble out on deck to the rescue.

## V.I.P's INSPECTION

Inspecting the beaches Admiral Ramsay seems content with the Navies' progress while Air Chief Marshal Tedder instinctively glances up for signs of aerial activity. Admiral Ramsay was the Commander-in-Chief of all Naval operations while Air Chief Marshal Tedder was deputy to General Eisenhower throughout the entire operation.

**THE UNWANTED.** Beaten into submission by the tremendous pounding they had taken from the R.A.F. and Naval guns, the prisoners above were only too willing to volunteer and lend a hand unloading vehicles from an L.c.T. They are a mixed bunch, some sullen and tough, others young and dejected. Those on the left surrendered to the Americans in the Cherbourg area where they were over-run by the swift advance of General Bradley's U.S. troops up the Cotentin peninsula.

# "EVERY FOOT..

ALERT FOR ACTION a trio of Ulster Riflemen move cautiously forward on a patrol near Caen.

... of ground the enemy lost at Caen was like losing ten miles anywhere else." EISENHOWER.

AFTER the first five days of dour 'bashing on' inland from the beaches the leading brigades of the British 2nd Army came up against the hard crust of the German defence. Tough, veteran Panzer troops fought back with an almost fanatical courage and fury, completely confident of an ultimate Nazi victory.

At each British thrust forward enemy guns opened up on S.O.S. tasks, shells churning up the ground until it looked as though it had been ploughed. The whole front was a criss-cross of machine gun fire and, all the time, mortar bombs rained down—not singly but in numbers fired from multi-barrelled weapons.

The way ahead was impassable and the advance eased to a halt.

To the men of the 3rd, 50th, 6th Airborne and 3rd Canadian Divisions there was one order—" Dig in ! "

North of Caen the scene was set for the battle of Europe where the might of

DOUBLE UP THERE ! Snipers are still active as forward troops dash along the Tilly-Caen road to consolidate a newly-won position.

**ASSAULT COURSE.** An infantry section pause to make a quick recce before advancing over shattered tank obstacles.

the German Panzers was to batter itself to destruction against the unyielding positions of General Dempsey's British Liberation Army.

General Montgomery's object was to pin down the enemy armour, envelop it, and then ' write it off ' once and for all —not merely push it back to fight another day.

His handling of the battle was masterly. The constant aggressive pressure of the British tanks and infantry forced the enemy to throw all his troops into the battle, leaving none in reserve to build up a striking force. This left the American First Army free to attack Cherbourg and, subsequently, break out of the lodgement area.

Dug in, the 2nd Army kept up the offensive. Day and night patrols went out ; patrols that moved forward under cover silently, fought sudden violent actions, and returned, leaving the enemy with nerves constantly taut, never knowing when or where the next attack would strike.

Yet the Nazis fought back with a fury tainted with terror. Many had been told that if they were captured they would be shot. One group of prisoners ordered to dig slit trenches for their own protection knelt to plead—they thought they were to dig their own graves.

Day in and day out across the same pitted ground the battle raged, always growing in intensity as more men, guns and tanks came into action.

Behind the front the vast build-up progressed turning the whole area back to the beaches into a vast store dump and reserve. The 15th Scottish and 51st Highland Divisions came in . .

**THE BATTLEFIELD.** Smoke continually rises as the bitterest fighting in the campaign is waged in the area between Caen and the beaches.

**OLD ENEMIES.** Led by the skirl of the pipes, infantrymen of a Highland Regiment move up to resume where they left off fighting Rommel in the desert.

**MINEN.** In the frenzy of battle the enemy had no time to remove signs marking minefields.

**TANK HARBOUR.** After days and nights of desperate fighting, tank crews ' kip down '.

**KNOCKED OUT.** Its turret askew, a Panther burns, hit during a counter attack.

**MOPPING UP.** In the dust of an advancing tank, infantry press on remorselessly through a shattered village. (*Left*) A young Nazi sneers defiance even after capture.

the 7th and 11th Armoured, the 49th, the 2nd Canadian . . . division after division moved up to hold the Panzers.

The Germans too drew up all the available reinforcements from all over western Europe and, despite the repeated attacks of the R.A.F. and the activities of the Maquis, as June turned to July seven Panzer Divisions were in action on the British sector.

At the front, in the midst of a raging inferno, the infantry stood firm against the Panzer onslaughts. They fought, 'brewed up', wrote home; wondered when the post was coming up, and why 'their blinking unit' hadn't been mentioned in the papers or by the B.B.C.

There was humour. Like the Piat team who crawled to within fifty yards of a German position where the enemy were queuing up for breakfast. They didn't know what damage their Piat bomb had done—they hadn't waited to find out. But they swore they'd seen it hit a huge tureen and " cover half the German Army in porridge ".

All the while the Navy pumped shells into Caen which was plastered by thousands of tons of R.A.F. bombs.

The days turned into weeks. The Panzers attacked with increasing ferocity but the infantry held firm in their slit trenches just waiting . . . waiting for the order to get out and bash on forward.

**ADVANCE PATROL.** Grimly, Canadian infantry advance clearing snipers from a shell-torn street of a village near Caen.

**BATHING PARADE.** R.Es. engaged in building a bridge near Reviers have a short break to take a well-earned bathe in the sunshine.

**TEN MINUTE HALT.** Advancing infantry take a brief rest before pressing on into the bitter fighting round Caen while behind the front, Corps troops don't forget the Derby and a ' book ' is opened. The winner : Ocean Swell quoted on the board here at 40—1.

**AFTERMATH.** Just behind the 50th Division front, the M.O. treats a stretcher case while, nearby, prisoners are searched before being sent to the rear.

**MOVING UP.** On his scout car Brigadier Prior Palmer, commander of the 27th Armoured Brigade gives directions to his staff captain before touring units engaged with the Panzers.

**ALLIED CHIEFS.** Smiling confidently as they leave a conference marquee are Air Chief Marshal Tedder, General Eisenhower and, on his own home ground, General Montgomery.

# Nurse! NURSE!

"DON'T worry. You're going to be all right."

On a stretcher a young soldier opened his eyes, the pain in them banished for a moment by surprise. It was a nurse—a British nurse! But already she was leaning over the next man, cool, efficient and reassuring.

Twenty-four hours earlier the nurse had not been well herself—she was violently sick in an open L.c.T. circling round off the Mulberry harbour waiting to land. It was late; enemy planes bombed the shore as a yell came from the harbour: "No more unloading tonight."

Back went the reply: "We've eighty-one Nursing Sisters aboard."

There was more waiting, the L.c.T. circled, more nurses were sick, then permission was given to land. Weak and weary they clambered ashore to sink on the sand dunes and wait for their transport.

So the Army nurses landed in France.

There was no time to recover from the journey. They moved up at once across the shell-torn countryside to the hospitals set up in tents, marquees and shattered buildings just behind the front.

Even as the canvas went up and the stores were unpacked there were wounded to be treated. They were tired, gaunt and unshaven, some on stretchers, some limping, others, their eyes bandaged, were led in with infinite gentleness.

The pain of their wounds eased by drugs, the men were cheerful, their only need "a fag". Each man knew that everything that could possibly be done for him was being done.

EASY . . . EASY NOW. It hurts a bit but there is comfort in the gentle care of the W.A.A.F. nursing corporal—besides, he'll soon be home getting the best treatment possible.

In the marquees, turned into hot-houses by the June sun, the nurses worked swiftly and efficiently, always giving relief and comfort. Clothes were cut away, wounds dressed, and injections given. On every man there was a large label on which was written the treatment he had received so there could be no duplication.

Always above the sharp tang of antiseptics there was a heavy sweet smell—the stench of battle wounds.

A few miles ahead columns of smoke rose, and there were the noises of battle as the bitter fighting continued round Caen.

In jeeps, trucks and ambulances, the wounded came back. They were given penicillin, operated on and—when they could be moved—sent back to England.

From D plus 7, when the first Dakotas touched down in Normandy, the R.A.F. Casualty Evacuation Units worked in close liaison with the Army hospitals.

Immediately they learned that a flight of transport planes were to land in the bridgehead, the R.A.F. Units contacted the hospitals, said how many patients they anticipated the aircraft would be able to carry, and subsequently collected the wounded in ambulances and carried them to the airstrips without any delay.

**THE ROAD BACK.** Sister Tomlinson (*left*) waded ashore waist deep in the sea in a hospital advance group. Walking wounded march back through a deserted village to the beach. They've seen death face to face and come back like soldiers—in step.

**STORES CHECK.** Army nursing sisters check clean sheets and blankets. The day after they landed they were taking in patients in hospitals of tents and marquees.

**" STEADY MATE."** Half a mile away his comrades crawl on their bellies towards the enemy positions. Now, brought from the front on a jeep, the wounded man is helped into a shattered building where the Regimental Aid Post has been set up. (*Left*) Exhausted and unshaven after days of battle a wounded man finds affection.

**IT WON'T BE LONG NOW.** Walking wounded rest against the side of an ambulance waiting for the plane that will fly them back to England. W.A.A.F. nursing orderlies hand out the unfailing treatment—a ' brew up '.

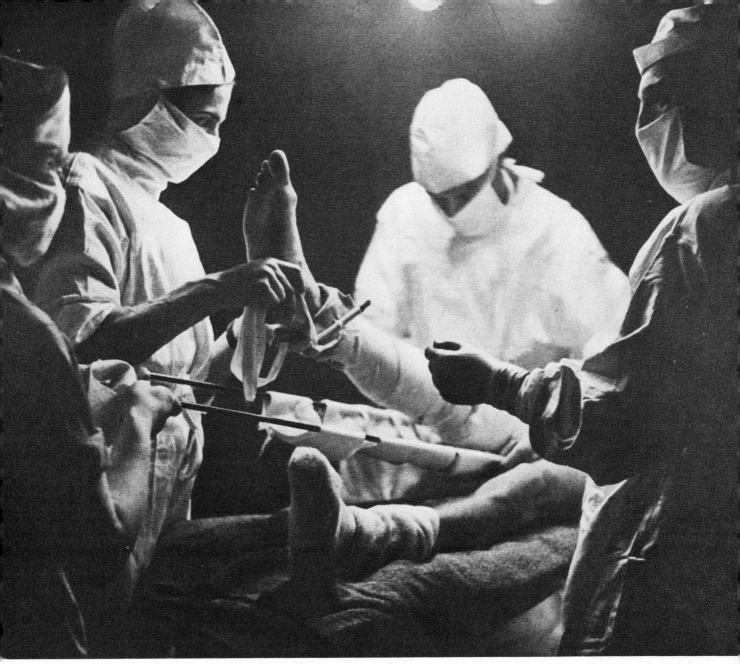

**"SPLINT, NURSE."** In a marquee naked bulbs glow as a surgeon sets a shattered leg; the nursing sister holds the splint ready. The operation over, the patient is flown home.

The transport aircraft were not specifically for carrying wounded, their main task being to bring supplies into the bridgehead, but, whenever possible, W.A.A.F. nursing orderlies were put aboard to look after the patients on the return flight.

From Normandy the aircraft took the wounded to the R.A.F. hospital at Roughton from which they were redirected to hospitals all over the North of England.

By the end of July over 10,000 patients had been flown home by the R.A.F. But the wounded kept coming back and the doctors, nurses and evacuation units never spared themselves . . . day and night they worked, operating, injecting, dressing wounds and giving comfort.

To them there is no memorial—their memory is preserved in the men who came back to live.

**ALERT.** The location of the gun site is protected by Ack Ack guns, the gunners of which are constantly on the alert for enemy aircraft although the Luftwaffe very seldom came over.

**FIRE POWER.** Behind the infantry, 105 mm self-propelled guns fire incessantly to blast a way for the American infantry fighting their way doggedly across the Cherbourg peninsula.

AFTER the first bloody baptism of fire on Omaha beach, General Bradley's First American Army fought back savagely and rapidly enlarged their bridgehead.

It was violent, bitter fighting, the enemy observing to the letter Hitler's order that 'every man shall fight and fall where he stands'. They fought—and they fell. In the first week of this desperate encounter there were tens of thousands of casualties as the G.Is. kept up the pressure, probing, thrusting, advancing—southwards towards Ste. Lo, and westwards to throw a cordon right across the Cotentin peninsula.

While the close 'bocage' country of tall hedges, banks, woods, and streams proved tough going to veterans of the 50th T.T. and 51st Highland Divisions who were used to manoeuvring in the vastness of the desert, to the American General 'Joe' Collins it was like fighting in his own back yard. Previously he had commanded a division fighting the Japanese in the dense jungle of Guadalcanal, which made the French 'bocage' seem like open country.

By D plus 17 he had virtually sealed off the Cotentin peninsula and the 4th, 9th and 79th Divisions swung northwards towards the first major port available to the Allies—Cherbourg.

Urgency was added to the attack on this front by the complete wrecking of the American Mulberry harbour off St. Laurent during the great storm on D plus 13.

Eagerly the Americans thrust northwards advancing on narrow fronts and disdaining any threats to their flanks. Never did the pace slacken.

Hitler fumed that Cherbourg must be held at all costs, but already von Schlieben, the garrison commander, had seen the writing on the wall.

As the American advance moved swiftly northwards right across the 30-mile front, units from the garrison were despatched to try to stem the advance—but to no avail. Often alone, without tanks or artillery support, the U.S. infantry fought viciously to overrun one defence line after another, until in less than five days from the beginning of the attack north they were within three miles of the port facing the vast concrete emplacements, anti-tank ditches, the wire and mines—Cherbourg's last line of defence.

The depleted garrison defence consisted of the badly mauled remnants of four divisions, Luftwaffe and Navy personnel, and workers on the V.1. site. A motley, bedraggled force, yet

**CLOSE COUNTRY.** G.Is. have to get out and push their jeep through a mud pack to reach their unit. In the close 'bocage' country fighting was from hedgerow to hedgerow.

**PARATROOP PATROL.** American paratroops move stealthily through a French village which has not been cleared of snipers. Every bush, wall, window was a hiding place for the enemy.

they stood firm and, after von Schlieben refused to surrender on June 21, it took three days of stiff—and often hand-to-hand — fighting before the fanatical defence was smashed and Cherbourg entered.

Even when captured, the German commander refused to order the surrender of the naval forts and the Arsenal which were still holding out.

To the Arsenal, a vast concrete emplacement obviously impregnable to bombs and shells, General Collins brought up a loud-speaker van to talk to the defenders. Under a white flag an envoy from the German commander came out and inferred that while the Arsenal commander could not be talked into surrender, the situation would, of course, be different if they were fired upon. Obligingly the Americans fired a few rounds, a white flag again appeared, and the defenders trooped out into captivity, their honour satisfied.

For a few days the harbour forts held out but Cherbourg had fallen. The Allies had gained a major Atlantic port.

**FIRE !** The order is given and another shell fired to soften up the defences of Cherbourg before the infantry advance.

**MESSAGE IS RECEIVED.** Swiftly signallers note map references as the forward infantry call for more artillery support.

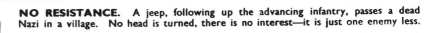

**NO RESISTANCE.** A jeep, following up the advancing infantry, passes a dead Nazi in a village. No head is turned, there is no interest—it is just one enemy less.

**NEARLY THERE.** A jeep pauses in Montebourg—20 miles ahead is Cherbourg.

**TO THE VICTOR . . .** nothing but rubble. Over a track jeeps bump into Saint Lo, scene of the bitterest fighting in the American sector.

**CHERBOURG.** A sunken ship almost blocks the inner harbour, but behind there is peace. Cherbourg is in the hands of the U.S. Army.

GUNS were towed into position, ammunition trucks came up, tanks rattled and roared across wheatfields to support the infantry ; each move devoured petrol, petrol by the thousands of gallons, yet there was no shortage—there was PLUTO.

This was one of the greatest triumphs of ' the back-room boys ' besides being one of the best kept secrets of the war.

As early as 1942 a network of pipe lines, 1,000 miles long, was constructed to carry petrol brought across the Atlantic to the relatively safe ports of the Mersey and Bristol Channel to London and the South and East coasts. The invasion posed the problem of continuing the line under the sea to France.

The experts got to work and, after numerous tests, a pipe of 3 ins. diameter was approved. The manufacture of the 710 nautical miles required for PLUTO was commenced, and R.Es. and R.A.S.C. troops were trained to operate the pumps which were camouflaged as garages, bungalows and tea shops.

Special ships were needed with large holds to carry the huge heavy coils of pipe line ; barges were needed to join the main line to the beaches. All were made available and by D-Day the PLUTO Force had over a hundred officers and a thousand ratings.

Once Cherbourg had fallen and sea lanes had been cleared through minefields, a submarine pipe line was laid from the Isle of Wight and petrol was pumped over. Later, as the British and Canadian Corps moved north along the coast, more lines were laid across the Channel until the point was reached when over a million gallons of petrol a day passed through PLUTO to the Allied Armies in France.

# PLUTO
## Pipe Line Under The Ocean

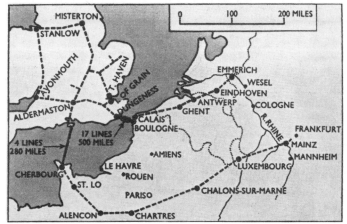

**PLUTO IS LAID.** From H.M.S. *Sancroft* the pipe-line rushes over the stern roller into the Channel at five knots. Careful watch is kept and the sailor with headphones and microphone is in constant contact with the ship's Chief Engineer.

**CONTROL ROOM.** At Dungeness Captain Hutchins, R.N. with Major Danger and Captain Gordon, both of the R.A.S.C., study the plan which shows the amount of spirit being pumped through each pipe-line across the Channel.

**FIRST—LAST.** Lieut. Griffiths, R.N.R., 1st lieutenant of the *Sancroft* cuts the rope as the last length goes overboard.

**LAST LINK.** The tug *Britannic* joins up the main 27-mile pipe from England to her own 2-mile length to complete the 27th pipe-line to France.

# CAEN FALLS

**BEFORE DAWN.** 4.5 guns hurl death into the stricken town. *(Below)* Men of the Durham Light Infantry use local transport as they move up a dusty road towards the front.

ONLY Hitler cheated General Dempsey of a victory at Caen at the end of June.

Then, after the breakthrough by the XXX and VIII Corps between Tilly and Caen, which culminated in the 15th Scottish Division gaining a salient over the Odon, Caen was virtually outflanked.

Hausser, the German commander in the field proposed moving back from the town which he maintained was untenable, and Rommel advised Hitler that he wished to make withdrawals to a firmer line of defence. But the Fuhrer was adamant and refused to listen. He ordered Caen to be held—and thereby doomed the Panzers to ultimate destruction in General Montgomery's trap. They had no further opportunities of making an orderly withdrawal.

Each day the British held the Panzers at Caen, the Americans secured fresh ground and were building up swiftly ready for the break-out that was to lead to the Falaise pocket—destined to be the graveyard of the cream of the Wehrmacht.

With Hitler's order for the city to be held the fury of the battle rose to a new peak of violence and ferocity. The Fuhrer had ordered a court martial enquiry into the capitulation of Cherbourg. The inference was obvious—there was no question of retreat.

In their slit trenches, the men of the British 2nd Army stood firm. Even as tanks and flame-throwers overran their positions they held out until anti-tank guns dealt with the enemy.

The morale of the troops was enormously high, they were itching to clamber out of the trenches and advance but, as yet, they had to sit tight and hold.

This was the period when the gunners dominated the battlefield. Day and night they continued to pound away at the enemy, at times each gun on the front firing over a hundred rounds in twenty-four hours.

Any advance was costly. As part of a feint to hold the enemy while the thrust was made over the Odon to the west, the 3rd Division made limited advances and, in the 8th Brigade's sector, the South Lancs advanced silently at night to take a chateau at La Londe, north of Caen.

At dawn the enemy counter-attacked with tanks and, without anti-tank guns in action, the South Lancs were forced to withdraw.

A few days later they again attacked in the evening with tremendous gallantry, but the Panzers fought back so viciously that, once again the Lancashiremen were forced back from the chateau, but clung to positions in a nearby wood.

In the early hours of the following morning the Suffolks and East Yorks took up the attack. It was still the

CLOSING IN. As a squadron of tanks advance to meet the Panzers, signallers lay lines. The battle is on.

FIRE! A "crocodile" sends a terrifying wave of flaming death on to a lonely farm house which is suspected of holding a nest of enemy snipers.

**OLD SCORE.** Hidden by leaves, a sniper of the French Resistance keeps watch for enemy movement below in the orchard.

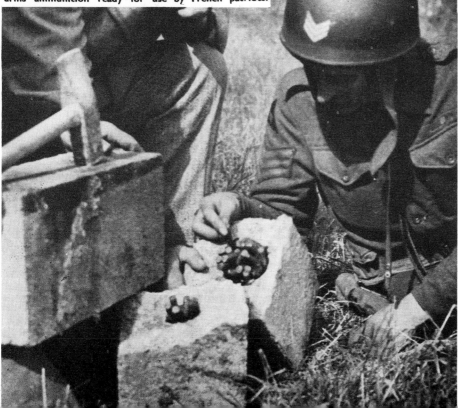

**MAQUIS SECRET.** A 3rd Division sergeant watches as a kerbstone is broken open to reveal a core of small arms ammunition ready for use by French patriots.

twilight of dawn as they moved forward and the air was laden with dust thrown up by their supporting artillery.

The noise was ear-splitting, there was firing all round and, in the half-light, it was difficult to distinguish our own troops from the enemy.

The fighting was desperate and bloody ; the casualties heavy. But with the dawn the Nazis had withdrawn—those that were still alive. The 8th Brigade began to dig in.

While they were consolidating one Company was continually under fire from a Spandau on the flank and, seeing two tanks roll up, a Suffolks' officer ran over to the nearer one to ask them to bring fire to bear on the machine-gun. Only when a head appeared from the turret did he realise the tank was a Panzer . . . as its gun swung round the officer ran like blazes to tumble into the safety of the nearest slit trench.

The resistance to this attack was so bitter that further 3rd Division attacks were for the time being cancelled.

It was not until the enemy attempted

to exert pressure on the American front that Montgomery decided the time was ripe to move in and take Caen and, with a tremendous bombing attack by the R.A.F. on the night of July 7th, the attack opened.

At dawn the advance began on a three-division front—the 3rd on the left, the 59th in the centre and the 3rd Canadian Division on the right.

The enemy fought desperately to hold every foot of ground, particularly in the centre where the 49th Division faced the 12th S.S. On the flanks the 3rd British and 3rd Canadians fared better and, by dusk, the former were on the fringe of the city.

Here it was not the enemy that checked them, but the fantastic rubble caused by the Navy shelling and R.A.F. bombing. However the following morning the advance battalion of the 9th Brigade—the Ulster Rifles—thrust into the centre of the town as the Canadians came in from the west.

Caen had fallen.

The enemy continued to stubbornly hold the factory area to the east and the suburbs of the city. These were only taken after operation 'Goodwood' when the 7th and 11th Armoured Divisions broke out east of Caen with the 2nd and 3rd Canadians on their right, and the 3rd British on their left.

This was the last phase of the Caen battle. The British 2nd Army had held, and defeated, the full might of Rommel's Panzers.

**UNDER COVER** of a line of trees, platoon headquarters of an infantry company moves up. In front are men laden with cases of mortar bombs with, trudging behind them, the mortar man.

**ARROWHEAD FORMATION.** Moving as though on an exercise, infantry go in to the attack.

**MARCH PAST.** Prisoners gape open-mouthed, their escorts are reassured and have added confidence . . . Monty is with them.

**BOMBS AWAY.** Leaving a wake of death and destruction, an R.A.F. bomber of the 2nd Tactical Air Force flies over a Caen factory.

**THEY'RE IN!** A Sherman of the Royal Canadian Armoured Brigade thunders into the desolate streets of Caen.

**FRONT LINE DOCTOR.** Bullets whine overhead as, a hundred yards from the enemy, a Canadian is treated for a head wound on the outskirts of Caen.

**AMEN.** The padre finishes the burial service. Silent around the grave, battle-worn tank men stand bareheaded to give solemn tribute to one of their comrades.

**CAEN AHEAD.** At Bretteville, southwest of Caen, lies the wreckage of what was a unit of the 21st Panzer Div.

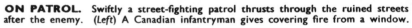

**ON PATROL.** Swiftly a street-fighting patrol thrusts through the ruined streets after the enemy. (*Left*) A Canadian infantryman gives covering fire from a window.

**THE ROAD IN.** Along a bomb-blasted track a tank struggles into the town. (*Left*) To the North prisoners roll in and are immediately searched for weapons.

**SCOTTISH BORDERERS** set up a captured Hotchkiss machine gun to help clear the remaining Nazi stragglers out of the town centre.

**TANK TRAP.** Lying hidden in the fallen masonry, a PIAT team are prepared for action against an enemy armoured counter attack.

**THE R.A.F. WERE HERE.** Wisps of smoke rise from still-smouldering buildings, there is no other movement . . . Caen has fallen.

# VICTORY

**MAY 4, 1945.** At his Tactical Headquarters on Luneburg Heath, just south of Hamburg, General Montgomery reads the surrender terms to General Admiral von Friedeburg and other representatives of the German High Command.

BENEATH a Union Jack fluttering proudly in the stiff breeze, representatives of the German High Command stood to attention and saluted General Montgomery as he emerged from his Tactical Headquarters on Luneburg Heath. It was May 4th, 1945 and they had come to surrender unconditionally to their conqueror.

Amid the rubble of Berlin, Hitler lay dead in an underground shelter, destroyed—like all else he had touched—by his own hand.

Everywhere along the British, Canadian and American fronts vast armies of weary dispirited troops were seeking to surrender.

In Bremen and Hamburg, in the British sector, long lines of prisoners trooped by and, occasionally, a truck-load of released British prisoners cheering wildly. At Station Hamburg there was no Lord Haw Haw with his " Gairmany calling . . ." It was Wynford Vaughan Thomas announcing : " This is Radio Hamburg, a Station of the Allied Military Government."

Meanwhile at Luneburg the German representatives sat round a table in a marquee. At the head General Montgomery began to speak :

" Now we've assembled here today to accept the surrender terms which have been made with the delegation from the German Army . . ."

The terms having been read through, the German representatives signed in order of seniority.

The following morning there would be peace on the British front.

Immediately signals were despatched to the British Divisions in the field :—

" RESTRICTED. Cancel all offensive ops forthwith and cease fire 0800 hrs. 5 May 45. Further details later."

A few days later, on May 7th at General Eisenhower's Headquarters in Rheims, the general surrender of all German forces on all fronts was signed before representatives of the United States, France, Britain and Russia.

The war in Europe was over.

<u>Instrument of Surrender</u>

of

<u>All German armed forces in HOLLAND, in</u>

<u>northwest Germany including all islands,</u>

<u>and in DENMARK.</u>

1. The German Command agrees to the surrender of all German armed forces in HOLLAND, in northwest GERMANY including the FRISIAN ISLANDS and HELIGOLAND and all other islands, in SCHLESWIG-HOLSTEIN, and in DENMARK, to the C.-in-C. 21 Army Group. *This to include all naval ships in these areas.* These forces to lay down their arms and to surrender unconditionally.

2. All hostilities on land, on sea, or in the air by German forces in the above areas to cease at 0800 hrs. British Double Summer Time on Saturday 5 May 1945.

3. The German command to carry out at once, and without argument or comment, all further orders that will be issued by the Allied Powers on any subject.

4. Disobedience of orders, or failure to comply with them, will be regarded as a breach of these surrender terms and will be dealt with by the Allied Powers in accordance with the accepted laws and usages of war.

5. This instrument of surrender is independent of, without prejudice to, and will be superseded by any general instrument of surrender imposed by or on behalf of the Allied Powers and applicable to Germany and the German armed forces as a whole.

6. This instrument of surrender is written in English and in German. The English version is the authentic text.

7. The decision of the Allied Powers will be final if any doubt or dispute arises as to the meaning or interpretation of the surrender terms.

B. L. Montgomery
Field-Marshal

4 May 1945
1830 hrs..

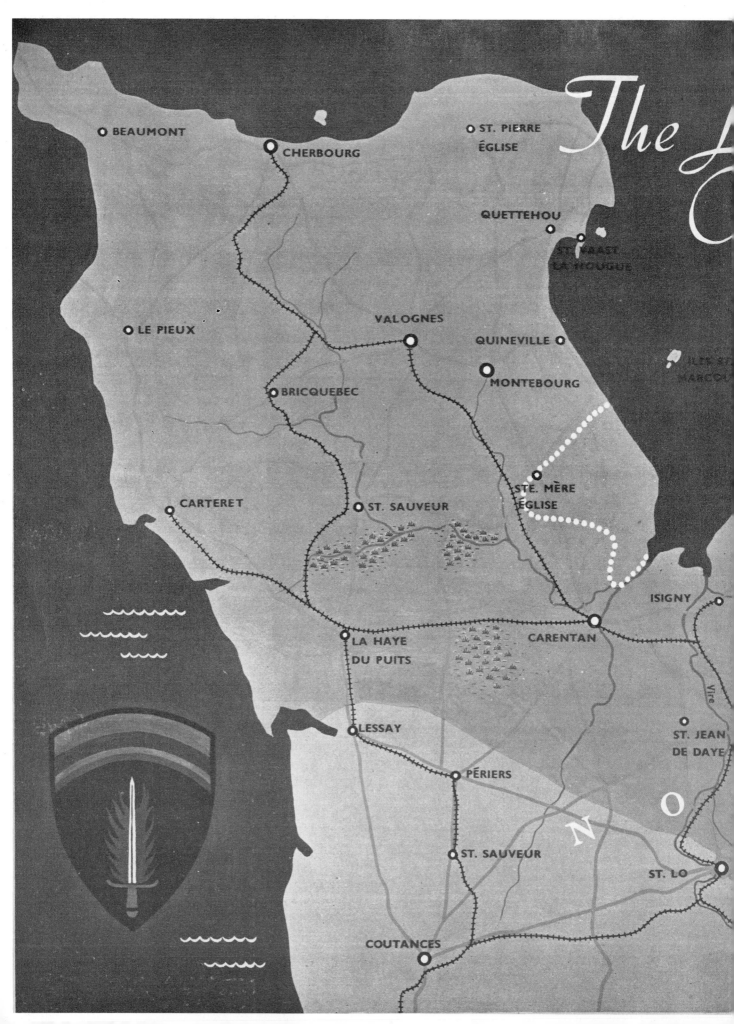

O BEAUMONT

CHERBOURG

O ST. PIERRE
ÉGLISE

*The* ~~*E*~~

QUETTEHOU

ST. VAAST
LA HOUGUE

VALOGNES

QUINEVILLE

O LE PIEUX

MONTEBOURG

BRICQUEBEC

ILES ST.
MARCOU

STE. MÈRE
ÉGLISE

CARTERET

O ST. SAUVEUR

ISIGNY

LA HAYE
DU PUITS

CARENTAN

LESSAY

ST. JEAN
DE DAYE

PÉRIERS

N

O

ST. SAUVEUR

ST. LO

COUTANCES

## lodgement
## completed

This map shows the expansion from the D-Day bridgeheads marked in white, to the complete establishment of the lodgement area. This was after operation 'Goodwood' in the last week of July, 1944. At this phase the full weight of the German armour was held by the British and Canadians around the Caen area. With this firm pivot the Americans were freed to break out, close the Falaise pocket, and thrust right into the heart of France.

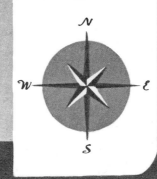

N
W          E
S

Seine Bay

RANDCAMP

LA CAMBE

FORMIGNY

TRÉVIÈRES

PORT-EN-BESSIN

ARROMANCHES

LA RIVIÈRE

CREULLY

LION

DOUVRES

HERMANVILLE

Pegasus Bridge

BAYEUX

Caen Canal

Orne

RANVILLE

BALLEROY

TILLY

CARPIQUET

CAEN

TROARN

M        A        N        D        Y

BOURGUÉBUS

EVRECY

CAUMONT

VILLIERS

BRETTEVILLE

TORIGNI

AUNAY